OETIC PROPHETIC DEVOTIONAL

I0081105

HE

leads

ME

MAVE MOYER

He Leads Me
Copyright © 2020—Mave Moyer
ALL RIGHTS RESERVED

Unless otherwise noted, all scripture references are from *The Holy Bible, New International Version*, copyright © 1973, 1978, 1984, 2011 by Biblica, Colorado Springs, Colorado. References marked KJV are from the *Holy Bible, King James Version*, public domain. References marked ESV are from the *The Holy Bible, English Standard Version*, copyright © 2001 by Crossway Bibles, a publishing ministry of Good News Publishers. References marked NLT are from *The Holy Bible, New Living Translation*, copyright © 1996, 2004, 2007 by Tyndale House Foundation. Used by permission of Tyndale House Publishers, Inc., Carol Stream, Illinois. References marked NASB are from the New American Standard Bible, copyright © 1960, 1962, 1963, 1968, 1971, 1972, 1973, 1975, 1977 by the Lockman Foundation, La Habra, California. References marked ASV are from *The American Standard Version of the Bible*, Public Domain. References marked MSG are from *The Message*, copyright © 1993, 1994, 1995, 1996, 2000, 2002 by NavPress Publishing Group, Colorado Springs, Colorado. References marked NKJV are from *The Holy Bible, New King James Version*, copyright © 1979, 1980, 1982, 1990 by Thomas Nelson, Inc., Nashville, Tennessee.

Published by:

McDougal & Associates
18896 Greenwell Springs Road
Greenwell Springs, LA 70739
www.thepublishedword.com

McDougal & Associates is an organization dedicated to the spreading the Gospel of the Lord Jesus Christ to as many people as possible in the shortest time possible.

ISBN: 978-1-950398-27-0

Printed on demand in the U.S., the U.K. and Australia
For Worldwide Distribution

Contents

Introduction

Ephesians 5:18-20, ESV

> And do not get drunk with wine, for that is debauchery, but be filled with the Spirit, addressing one another in psalms and hymns and spiritual songs, singing and making melody to the Lord with your heart, giving thanks always and for everything to God the Father in the name of our Lord Jesus Christ.

The poetic prophetic psalm...the poetic prophetic...the new song...the prophetic song of the Lord are all forms of intimate communication. They are the sound and the song of an open and yielded heart to the Lord.

The poetic prophetic comes from the heart of love that God has for us. He will speak words to bring comfort and grace and direction and correction in love and compassion as He sends a poetic psalm to our hearts.

Through the prophetic song, God will reveal His heart to us...and sing over us and strum the strings of our heart...playing a melody of grace in our lives. God sings a love song into our hearts, and we respond to His love.

The song of the Bride sings back in response to the Lord. It is a freely-expressed spiritual song adoring and loving the Bridegroom. Gratitude and thanksgiving for His constant care and involvement in our lives...flows.

Psalm 98:1, NIV

> Oh sing to the Lord a new song,
>> for he has done marvelous things!
> His right hand and his holy arm
>> have worked salvation for him.

The new song is a song of deliverance...a song that brings change.
It's a song of victory and overcoming.
A new song...brings a new day.
It's a song that reminds us that God is always with us.

These venues of gifting have great edifying power...and can be a spiritually intense avenue of ushering in the Glory of God.

1 Corinthians 2:9, KJV

Eye hath not seen, nor ear heard, neither have entered into the heart of man, the things which God hath prepared for them that love him.

When we will recognize His leadership and prophetic orchestration,
It will turn a key to entering into the Spirit.

As we learn to flow with Him...and allow Him to move...
There will be an intimate anointing released
To bless all who hear.

Lord, let Your glory fall in this place.
Let us know the fullness of Your grace.
And as we stand confessing...
Flow over us...like a canopy of blessing.

Lord, be in the banners...the flags...and the shout.
Be with us in the dance.. That's what worship's all about...
Yielding all of me...to the fullness of Your heart...
Offering my life in its fullness...not just in part.

To see Your spirit move and flow...
And to follow after You...
Releasing what You say...
And doing what I see You do.

Lord, rise in my work.
Rise also in my play.
Sit upon the throne of my life...
Each and every day.

Lord, fully move in me...
By the power of Your grace.
Come and take me deeper...
Into the secret place.

It is so wonderful the ways we hear God speak today.
He is always pouring out over us
And assuring us of His love and His constant care
And commitment.

I pray that the words penned in this devotional will bless you
And open your heart to hear God in new ways
And in deeper dimensions of His love.

Mave Moyer

A BE Attitude

Matthew 5:1-11, NIV

Now when Jesus saw the crowds, he went up on a mountainside and sat down. His disciples came to him, and he began to teach them. He said:

"Blessed are the poor in spirit,
     for theirs is the kingdom of heaven.
Blessed are those who mourn,
     for they will be comforted.
Blessed are the meek,
     for they will inherit the earth.
Blessed are those who hunger and thirst for righteousness,
     for they will be filled.
Blessed are the merciful,
     for they will be shown mercy.
Blessed are the pure in heart,
     for they will see God.
Blessed are the peacemakers,
     for they will be called children of God.

Blessed are those who are persecuted because of righteousness,
  for theirs is the kingdom of heaven.
"Blessed are you when people insult you, persecute you and falsely say all kinds of evil against you because of me.

The Lord said...

It's not about you...
It's about Me...
It's about you becoming...
Who I've called you to be.

In the Kingdom of Heaven...
We should not scar another's heart.
When we come together...
We should never tear apart.

Always we should shine His light...
Everywhere and every place.
We are not called to judge...
We are called to walk in grace.

Blessed are the poor in spirit...
Who confess and feel regret.
Blessed are those who show mercy...

Who forgive and forget.

Blessed are those who mourn...
For their comfort shall be in Me.
Blessed are the pure in heart...
For it's My face they'll see.

Blessed are the peacemakers...
Who will "in God"...bring compromise.
Blessed are those who hunger and thirst...
And humbly apologize.

Blessed are the meek...
They shall inherit the earth.
Their attitudes and actions...
Speak of God's matchless worth.

Blessed are the persecuted...
As they stand for Me...
Reflecting My character...
And My personality.

God's interested in our heart...
God is creating in us a new heart...
A "pure in heart," "sincere, without hypocrisy
and with nothing hidden.

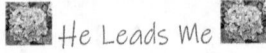

Pure in heart ... "What you see is what you get!"

Let's have a heart that forgives and refuses
To hold things in...or keeps a grudge alive,
A heart that's forthright and honest,
Asking the hard questions,
With the desire to make things better.

May His attitude...BE MY ATTITUDE!

Be of Good Courage

Psalm 27:14, KJV

> Wait on the LORD: be of good courage, and he shall strengthen thine heart: wait, I say, on the LORD.

We can only be courageous
By having faith and confidence in
The truth that God is with us and for us.
Not only does such confidence inspire courage,
But it dispels our fears.
Jesus, who is God in the flesh, admonishes us
Not to be afraid, but to believe in Him.
He said, *"Let not your hearts be troubled.*
Believe in God; believe also in me."

True courage rises up through believing
That God is with us and for us...
Father, Son, and Holy Spirit
And that nothing can separate us from
The love of God in Jesus Christ, our Lord.
It takes courage to love

When we've been hurt...
And when we've suffered pain.
It takes courage to forgive..
And try once again.

It takes courage and strength...
To walk through each day...
To face the hurdles and obstacles...
That stand in our way.

We encounter heartaches...
We suffer loss and grief...
But we press on in faith...
Holding fast to belief.

It takes courage to love...
When hurtful words are spoken.
It takes courage to trust...
When our heart's been broken.
Courage is firm...
And courage is gentle.
Courage is tough...
And it's sentimental.

Courage can conquer...
And yet it will surrender.
Courage is strong...
And, at times, it is tender.

Courage stands steadfast...
Not willing to doubt.
It takes courage to fit...
And to stand out.

In life...we will have struggles.
Let's not let our love wax cold.
Courage takes a chance.
It's resilient and it's bold.

Let's have courage to share our love...
And not let pride get in the way.
All of God's creations...
Have value to Him every day.

They are always worthy.
He loves in spite of all they've done.
So, let's follow the example...
Of God's precious Son.

God gives us the courage to truly love...
To stand with and weather the storms of life.
The reward of love is love itself.
And joy is always in the heart of the one who loves.

We all need the courage to love with no strings attached,
And in spite of the reaction or response of others.
God, help us today to walk in all Your ways...
In Your goodness and Your grace...
Bringing transformation every place.

Be Still

Psalm 46:10, NIV

> He says, "Be still, and know that I am God;
>> I will be exalted among the nations,
>> I will be exalted in the earth."

Be still and know that I am God...
I have heard your plea.
Surrender to My peace.
I will set your spirit free.

You are Mine...I've chosen you.
Do not be dismayed...
I have all things in My hand.
There's no need to be afraid.

In the midst of all the darkness...
I AM your Guiding Light.
I AM your ever present Help.
You are precious in My sight.

My love will be your anchor.
By your side I'll always stay.
I will be your strength and shield...
As you walk in My way.

In the midst of the troubles...
The storms and the floods...
No evil will befall you.
You are covered by My blood.

Though Satan seeks destruction...
I will touch and make you whole.
Of My living water you shall drink...
And satisfy your thirsty soul.

Be still and know that I am God...
I see each and every tear.
I know your deepest secrets...
I calm your deepest fear.

Be still and know I'm working...
To quiet every storm.
While I use each and every trial...
To strengthen and to form.

Be Still

My mercy is new every morning...
My faithfulness is sure.
Be still and know I AM...GOD,
And by faith...you will endure.

Become

When the caterpillar has been changed into a butterfly...
It becomes what God always intended it to be.

God is in the transformation business, and He is determined
That we will all be like Jesus in the end.

Romans 8:29, ASV
> For whom he foreknew, he also foreordained to be
> conformed to the image of his Son, that he might be the
> firstborn among many brethren

Change will not happen by accident.
We must be intentional in our yielding.
It won't happen overnight.
We must persevere and be willing
To withstand the struggle of becoming.

Struggling is an important part of any growth experience.
In fact, without the struggle to emerge from the cocoon,
The butterfly will never fly.

Become

It's the struggle that strengthens her wings
And gives her the power to become.
In our lives, it is the struggle that creates us
And gives us the ability to become
The best version of who God called us to be.

God already knew the fruit our life would bear
And the struggles we would go through
In order to get us there.

None of this will happen without the Holy Spirit...
And our personal commitment...
To be accountable to the Lordship of Jesus.

Change me, Lord.
Let me be...
The kind of person...
You're expecting of me.

As I yield to your Spirit...
There's so much You can do.
You'll touch me and change me...
And make me brand new.

By the power of Your grace...
From the inside out...
As I press through by faith...
And let go of my doubt.

In the midst of the struggle...
The trials and tests...
I will emerge...
Favoured and blessed.

Change me, dear Jesus.
Make my heart true.
Help me to see the sin...
In the things I still say and do.

Touch me and show me...
The things I do wrong.
In the midst of my weakness...
Lord, show Yourself strong.

Here in Your presence...
I'll see You're all I need...
To live out Your life...
In my words and my deeds.

Through all of life's journey...
When I laugh...when I cry...

Become

You're there in the struggle...
To make sure I fly.

Becoming Like Him

What a tremendous comfort it is to know that
When we are suffering from the limitations
Of our bodies we have a High Priest who can
Sympathize with our weaknesses, and has
Been tempted in all things as we are,
Yet without sin (see Hebrews 4:15).

Jesus, fully human and fully divine.
He spoke the Word, and the winds ceased,
And the surging waves were instantly as smooth as glass.

Just as His humanity encourages us,
Because we know He understands,
His deity encourages us
Because He is powerful to act on our behalf.

Nothing is too difficult for our God.
Not a breath of wind or a drop of rain...
No trouble...no test...

No devil in Hell can defy His sovereign rule.
The closer we are to Him, the more intimately we know Him,
The more we can trust Him
In the trials and storms in life.

As we endure the storms of life by faith in Him,
We know...that He is always with us..
Through its troubles and its blows.

On the broken road we travel...
The Lord walks with me and you.
And in every trial and test...
He will bring us through.

He will change us through the trouble...
And comfort us in the pain.
He will heal us and renew us...
Like a sweet refreshing rain.

Both in times of joy and sadness...
When things are wrong and when they're right...
His love will lift us higher...
And fill us with His light.

He suffered...and was tempted.
He lived...to comprehend...

The things that we all go through.
He stands with us to the end.

We can always trust our Lord...
To meet our every need...
As we give ourself to You, God...
Our every word and every deed.

Make us more like Jesus.
Keep us always in God's will.
And by the power of Your Spirit...
Our earthly purpose we'll fulfill.

The Blessing of Children

Having children gives us real insight into how much God,
Our Father, loves us.
When I think about how much I love my children,
It's hard to pen words that could ever express it.
God loves us all more than that.
Being a parent helps us understand
Why God doesn't always jump in and bail us out
In the midst of difficult circumstances.
When we jump in and rescue our children
Every time they get into a challenging situation...
We are not preparing them to live in the real world.

Psalm 127:3, NIV

> Children are a heritage from the LORD,
>   offspring a reward from him.

Children are given to us directly from the hand of God.
They are gifts of grace sent from Heaven to Earth.
There is no pleasure in life that can equal

The pleasure of seeing our own children grow up.
So much like you, made in your image,
A miniature of you, yet so very different.
They might walk like you or talk like you,
They may have your sense of humour...
Yet they will have a mind of their own...
And a unique and special call of God for their lives.

Children bring God's love into our lives like nothing else. They
Are a little piece of heaven sent to us.
When we look into their eyes,
We know that only God could have created this little miracle.
Every child comes bearing the fingerprint of God.
It's a great pleasure...honour and responsibility to be a parent.

Jesus loves the little children...and so should we.

You're the song my heart is singing.
You're the poem my feelings write.
You're the masterpiece my memory paints...
And my star that's shining bright.

I've watched you change and grow...
As seasons quickly passed.
I thank God "He has a plan"...
And that my faith held fast.

Life is a journey that's short.
The seasons rush quickly by.
Before we know it...our kids grow up...
Right before our eyes.

They're no longer there beside us.
Their story books are put away.
No more fixing boo boos...
No more "Mommy, come and play."

No more prayers and tucking in...
With night-night kisses...again and again.
"I need some water"..."turn on my light."
Now it's quiet...at home...at night.

The sweetest thing's remembering.
You were both so little then.
Sometimes my heart can't help but wish...
That you were small again.

It hurt to see the heartaches...
You suffered as you grew.
But nothing broke your spirit.
God used it all to strengthen you.

Bitter sweet emotions...
Laughter...joy...and tears...
With gratitude and thankfulness...
I cherish all the years.

From the second that I held you...
I wished that I had known...
That the years would seem like minutes...
After you had grown.

There were times of pain and times of tears...
Days of faith and days of fears...
Building a love that bound our hearts...
Even when we're far apart.

All grown up and on your own...
You are God's...and mine on loan.
You fill my heart, and you'll always be...
The best thing in life that happened to me.

The Blessing of Family

Psalm 103:17-18, NIV

> But from everlasting to everlasting
>> the LORD's love is with those who fear him,
>> and his righteousness with their children's children—
> with those who keep his covenant
>> and remember to obey his precepts.

Family should be a safe place to mess up.
We need the ointment of grace
Applied to the wounds of our hearts at times.
We must remember that love, not perfection, is our goal.
Home should always be a place of retreat
Where we can find forgiveness...comfort, rest and healing.

In our families and our homes, we should always cultivate
An atmosphere tempered and flavoured with acts of kindness,
Mutual respect, humility, and love.
Every family member needs the "Son" to shine in our hearts.
We are all like a flawed masterpiece,

We can have external, visible beauty,
But far more importantly, we need to BE sincere
In our quest to be a good and godly place...
A family where healing and wholeness can be received.

When we allow His Spirit within us to have his way...
We will be without offence.
We will choose to love and continue to express
And display the grace of God every day...in every way.

A family is made of love and tears...
Sorrow and joy...throughout the years.
It grows stronger, as time quickly ticks by.
We learn to count on, trust and rely...
On imperfect people...who sometimes bring pain.
We learn how to love...and dance in the rain.

A family's a circle...of taking and giving.
They make life hard...and make it worth living.
Family are friends we're born to...
They are with us till the end.
God intended, when life would treat us rough...,
Our family...our heart would mend.

Although sometimes we fuss and fight.
And we may not always agree...

Forgiveness and grace will win the day.
I'll love you, and you'll love me.

I thank God for my Family Tree...
A place where love and grace abound.
Our roots are deeply planted in HIM...
A rich and fertile ground.

We enjoy the seasons of sunshine.
We endure the days of rain.
And when struggle and heartache visit...
Together we bear the pain.

God gave us this precious gift...
To love and treasure and cherish.
He intended that, at our life's end...,
No family bonds would perish.

There's so much to be thankful for...
All the memories, all the years...
Special times together...
Full of laughter...full of tears.

I thank God for where we are today...
That He's taken us under his wing...
And given us strength, support, and love...
That only a FAMILY can bring...

Lord, bless my family and children.
Give them hearts that love You and desire to follow You.
Give my family the strength to fear You
And not to be afraid of the things in the world around them.
Give them the courage to stand up to what is right...
And produce within them godly character
And an attitude of honesty and integrity.
May their lives bring You glory.

Lord, thank You for protecting every member
Under the shadow of Your wings.
Help us all to surrender to Your grace
And find our strength in You.
Increase our love and patience and kindness and goodness.
Help us to prefer one another...esteem each other
And speak well of each other.
Cause us to overflow with forgiveness...wisdom
And understanding, that we might become more like You.
And let unity and peace be the motivation
For all that we do.

Amen!

Communication Is Golden

Today we see that it's not just the traditions
And places of communication that have changed,
But also the desire and effort.

Communication is still so valuable and vital
For a healthy family.

Communication is a two-way street,
And we have to be committed to making it a top priority
In our lives.

When we communicate, let's smile
And look the other person in the eye...
Not stare them down.

Let's ask questions to show we are interested
And get clarification when there are things
We don't understand.
Don't assume.

Look for common ground
And put distractions on hold.

Don't focus on rehearsing what you'll say
When it's your turn...
While not hearing what is being said.

If the person expresses strong feelings,
Try to acknowledge them without taking it personal
And becoming offended or angry.

When used properly, words promote comfort...and healing
And they inspire understanding and encourage agreement.

When misused, they can aggravate, cause offence,
And drive us farther apart.

With God's help, we can improve our ability
To communicate the truth in a spirit of love,
Not the harsh truth, but the truth motivated through love.

Through loving and honest communication,
We can talk through concerns...suggest solutions,
And encourage new ways of thinking,
But we cannot force change.

If we speak the truth in love
And do all we can to care, as we confront the other person,
We will have succeeded in God's eyes,
Regardless of how the other person responds.

Colossians 4:6, NIV

Let your conversation be always full of grace, seasoned with salt, so that you may know how to answer everyone.

When communication...is the missing link...
We give the devil access...to the things we think.

As hard as communication can sometimes be...
To great relationships...it's the key.

When we're patient...and we're kind...
We can share our heart...and our mind.

If we're willing..in love to express...
We can clear up every mess.

Contentment

Lamentations 2:19, MSG

> As each night watch begins, get up and cry out in prayer.
> Pour your heart out face-to-face with the Master.

God does not expect us to "grin and bear it"
Or exercise toxic faith, denying that things are challenging.
But He honours our honest conversation and prayer
As we bear our heart and share our struggles...
And, by faith, trust that He is with us in every season.

If He brings us to it...He will bring us through it!

Contentment isn't denying our feelings
About wanting and desiring what we may not have.
But, instead, it exhibits a freedom
From being controlled by those feelings.

Contentment isn't pretending things are right
When they are not,

But, instead, it displays the peace that comes
From knowing that God is bigger than every problem,
And that He works them all out for our good.

Contentment isn't a feeling of well-being,
Contingent upon keeping circumstances under control,
But, instead, it promotes a joy in spite of circumstances,
Looking to God, who never changes.

Contentment is not based on external circumstances,
But, rather on an internal source.
Contentment comes from the heart
Fully given over to the Lord.

When we fail to fully surrender,
We will forever be discontented.
Our freedom will be suffocated
And we will be in bondage to our desires.
Our relationships will be poisoned
With jealousy and competition.
Potential blessings will be sacrificed.

Discontentment has the potential to disappoint us
From our appointment in God.
It destroys our peace, robs us of joy, make us miserable,
And can tarnish our witness.

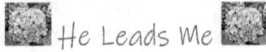

We dishonour God if we proclaim a Saviour who satisfies
And then live in discontentment.

God wants us to know that we are enough
And what we have is enough.
And, as we are faithful to give it to Him,
He will multiply it and continually provide for us.
Contentment comes from obedience to Him.

We are truly blessed to be content...
To be at peace...and satisfied...
To walk in love and gratitude...
Daily by His side.

A life well lived is a precious gift.
It makes the world a better place.
We can be content when we exercise...
Hope and strength and grace.

Life is filled with beautiful moments...
With smiles and sometimes tears.
We win, we lose, and rise again...
With joy and sorrow through the years.

Contentment comes from deep within...
No matter the blessing or plight.

Through our obedience to the Word...
Our faith will win the fight.

And we will run our race...
In the sunshine or the rain.
And we will overcome...
In the good times and the pain.

Content in the truth that He's with us...
That we never walk alone.
He is the Light in the darkness...
And there's no fear of the unknown.

A life well lived will be a legacy...
Of joy and pride and pleasure...
A lasting and lingering memory...
That we will value and treasure.

We will always overcome...
Because He overcame.
And we will learn to sing and dance...
Even in the rain.

Don't Grow Weary

Galatians 6:9, ESV

> And let us not grow weary of doing good, for in due season
> we will reap, if we do not give up.

We all have a mission...
A divine purpose in the earth...
Specially designed for us...
Long before our birth.

Some call it destiny...
The life we're appointed to.
It's there for us to walk out...
If we believe it's true.

It's planted in our heart by God...like seeds...it seems.
In time they grow, and fruit appears...
In the form of hopes and dreams.

But yet we still don't know...
All we are called to do.
But, as we listen with our heart...
He'll whisper it to me and you.

He fashioned us in the womb...
With purpose and with a plan.
He put a destiny in the heart...
Of every woman...every man.

He orders our every footstep.
The things we need...He'll give...
Just so the life He planned for us...
One day we will walk out and live.

So, dream the dreams He dreams.
Don't let them slip away.
The road may be rough and rocky...
But we'll arrive the appointed day.

If we don't grow weary in well doing...
Get distracted...disappointed or lost.
Keep pressing in...with all we have...
Going the distance, no matter the cost.

We owe our allegiance to our Father,
To BE...what we were born to be.
Let's press in and on and through it all...
To fulfill our destiny.

Drama Free

Matthew 5:16, NIV

In the same way, let your light shine before others, that they may see your good deeds and glorify your Father in heaven.

As we seek God's guidance
Through the ups and downs of life's drama,
Let's remember this message:

The best way to show the love of God
Is to live out the Word in our lives.
Let's show them instead of tell them.
Let's speak the truth in love
And not be afraid to set boundaries
And live our values and beliefs for all to see.
We can't fix anybody, but through watching us live...
They will see there is someone who can.

We will set an example of living a drama-free life.
Letting our light shine before others
Will glorify our heavenly Father...
And lead others to the goodness of His grace.

Love is always the star wherever it is given the stage.

Lord, we long to live...
A drama-free life...
Where patience and love...
Defeats troubles and strife...

A place where we're less angry...
More loving and giving...
Being an example to others...
By the life we are living.

Let us walk in Your peace...
In a life free of drama...
Leading others to healing...
In the places there's trauma.

Let us walk in Your Word...
Strong and consistent...
Loving others regardless...
Not being lukewarm and indifferent.

Let us not look down...
On those...broken and lost...
But remember to love like You loved...
No matter the cost...

Giving space and grace...
Treating all respectfully...
As my life peacefully shows them...
They can live drama free.

Drama free begins with you and me!

Experience His Presence

Psalm 16:11, NKJV

> In Your presence is fullness of joy;
> At Your right hand are pleasures forevermore.

James 5:8, NKJV

> Draw near to God and He will draw near to you.

Exodus 33:15, NKJV

> And He said, "My Presence will go with you, and I will give you rest."

Psalm 145:18, NKJV

> The LORD is near to all who call upon Him,
> To all who call upon Him in truth.

Come and relax in God's presence.
Let Him take your cares and burdens from you.
Take a few minutes and come into His rest...
And let His love and Spirit carry you.

Let Him refresh your spirit...
As you step through the portal of grace.
Enter the realm of His glory...
And...come and gaze into His face.

Here He will breathe new life...
And settle and calm your soul.
He takes your cares upon Himself.
Your perfecting is His goal.

Here He will share His thoughts...
And reveal His mysteries.
In the secret place of His heart...
He changes you and me.

So, we will become like Him...
In all we say and do.
He is longing for us to come away.
He loves "our presence" too.

He will touch our whole life...
Remaking me and you.
We won't even know ourselves...
When He is finally through.

He loves us, and He wants...
To give us His very best.
Our Father's always happy...
When His children all are blessed...

Can you feel His presence enveloping your soul?
The Holy Spirit is like a river. Feel Him flow.

On the inside of you and me...
Truly is the hope of Glory...
The fullness of the Godhead...the three in one...
Operating together...Father...Spirit and Son.

O my goodness, what a mystery...
The fullness of Heaven on the inside of you and me.

His presence is always with us...
So, all fear it has to go.
Our cares will be diminished...
When in His love we flow.

In His presence all the anxious thoughts...
Are stilled...and we are blessed.
New perspectives and mindsets emerge...
As we enter into rest.

Jesus said:

Do not worry about your life...
What you will eat or drink or wear.
Is life not more important than this?
Look at the birds of the air..
They do not sow or reap...
Or store away in barns, and yet...
Our heavenly Father feeds them.
And He will not forget.

Are you not much more valuable...
In each and every way?
Who of you by worrying...
Can add a single hour or a day?

And why do you worry about clothes?
See how the lilies of the field grow.
They do not labour or spin...
But look at the beauty they show.
Not even Solomon in all his splendour...
Was dressed like one of these.
If that is how God clothes the grass of the field...
Will He not much more...clothe you and me?

Do not worry about tomorrow...
Or the trouble it might bring.
Just put your eyes on Me...
And let your heart just sing.

Come and sit with Me here...
In the fullness of My grace...
In the realm of My presence.
Let's share...and reason together in this place.

Pray in the Spirit at "all times" and for every reason.
Stay alert and be "persistent...in each and every season.

I talk to Him. He talks to me.
I ask the question. He gives me eyes to see.
I open up my heart...to His purposes and plans...
And He pours out His wisdom for every nation...and land.

He truly cares about me...my desires and my needs.
He shows me how to reap the harvest...
Starting with the sowing of the seeds.
He leads me into all truth, showing me great things to come,
Always making me believe
That I am God's special someone!

He helps me in my weakness...
When I know not what to pray
With groaning and intercession.
Through me, He has His say.
For I cannot express in words the greatness of His plan,
So the Spirit makes His utterance through the heart of man.

He prays within us...when we let Him have His way...
The mysteries and purposes of God
Prayed out through us today.
So, as we work together...in relationship and faith...
We can trust Him always...to exercise His grace.

His grace...shall be sufficient for all we're going through.
His Spirit is wooing and calling me and you.
To come a little closer...to His fire and His flame...
And we will be forever changed. We'll never be the same.

As we pray "in the Spirit," building our most holy faith...
He will move us forward by the power of His grace.
He will strengthen us and fortify our future and our call.
As we spend a little time with Him...He will show us all.

All things pertaining to life and godliness...
And we will know the truth...and we surely will be blessed.
You see...His plan from the beginning

Included every provision, every rescue, every protection
That we would ever require.
Nothing is too big for Him.

Nothing is out of His jurisdiction or control.
No circumstance in our life is a surprise to Him.
He is never without a plan.

He is the Sovereign God who gave His life willingly for you
and me.

He committed to being our Father and to caring for us as His
children.

He will never leave us or forsake us.
His promise is true.
He is not a God who abandons His children.
He'll be there in all we do.

Consider His great love for us:

He created us with purpose
To be...His child...companion and friend.
He loves us just because He chooses to.
And with grace our hearts He tends.

We were created for the sole purpose
Of being loved by our radical relational God.
He's called us with a purpose.
With peace, our feet are shod.

We've been hand-picked to walk beside Him...
In His presence and His light.
He's given us His Spirit, so we can win this earthly fight.
I've called you by name.
I have called you Mine.
Time for my chosen ones...
To arise and shine!

I've crafted you in royalty...
To rule and reign with Me.
So, rise up and be...
A carrier of My glory.

I have made you beautiful...
Filled with love and light.
Arise and shine. The time has come.
Be pleasing in My sight.

Shine your light for others...
That they may look and see...

That the beauty that's inside you...
Is because you carry Me.

As you let your "life" house be My lighthouse.
As you move in all My ways...
You will change the lives of others...
And make a difference every day.

For the time is short. The time is NOW...
To arise. Step fully in.
Shine your light so others...
Can follow Me and win.

Day by day...the clock is ticking...
And many lives are cast away.
Arise and shine. Your light has come.
We are in the final days.

And as the darkness covers the earth
And people too...
We must make the decision.
It's up to me and you.

May the faithful Father enfold you with His amazing love.
May He wrap you in His peace that passes understanding.
May He pour out His hope and quicken your spirit
To receive His fullness now.

May Holy Spirit...show you, once again,
His incredible love and faithfulness.
May you walk through your days...
Wrapped in His loving presence...
Anticipating His amazing grace to be revealed
Over and over again...
One moment at a time...
As he takes your breath away...
With the knowledge of how important you are to Him.

When Jesus left Earth at His upward ascension...
There was one thing He just had to mention:
"Go into the world and tell them it's true,
That I love all of them... just like I love you."

There are so many others...
That He died for too.
They have a right to know Jesus
The way that we do.
May you know Him better...
Feel His presence more tangibly...
And flow in the river of His grace
More at the end of this day...
Than you did at the beginning.

May your life house become His lighthouse,
And may you shine with His grace.

When others see you, may they see His face.
May your words give them comfort
And your deeds lend a hand...
As you lead them into His presence
And to the Promised Land.

Faith for Life

Mark 11:23-24, ESV

Truly, I say to you, whoever says to this mountain, "Be taken up and thrown into the sea," and does not doubt in his heart, but believes that what he says will come to pass, it will be done for him. Therefore I tell you, whatever you ask in prayer, believe that you have received it, and it will be yours.

Faith can move a mountain...
And turn a river off its course.
Faith can win an impossible race.
It's a supernatural force.

Faith can change the circumstance...
And keep you standing till the end.
Faith takes you to a deeper place...
Where God's river ebbs and bends.

There, in His grace...,
Your faith is renewed.

And you'll know without doubt...
God is always with you.

No need to worry.
By faith, you will see...
Things will turn out
The way God wants them to be.
God's thoughts are higher...
And His ways...not like man's.
Faith rises above...
Our "reasoning" and plans.

Be faithful to trust Him.
He is walking with you.
He knows all that you need...
And He will come through.

He wants you to know...
As you trust in His ways...
He will meet your needs...
All of your days.

Don't look for solutions...
In the mind of a man.
Supernatural provision...
Is always His plan.

It's time to relax...
At peace...rest and stay...
And celebrate the blessing...
Of another day.

Faith in His Word

The first evidence of our faith is our words...
But the proof of our faith lies in our actions.
Our words will set the platform for us...
To walk out the promise...
But we have to walk it out.

Peter stepped out on the waves
Of a stormy and unsettled sea...
Because he moved on the spoken word, "COME."
That word from the Lord set the stage...
And gave Peter a platform to walk on.

It was only when Peter "considered"
The situation around him...that he fell to it.
But IF we can keep our eyes on Jesus...
And stay grounded and rooted "in His Word,"
We can walk our way out of and into
Everything God has called us to.

Without works, our faith is dead.

We must exercise our faith if we expect to receive from God.

Once we "hear," we must move.

Our words set the stage...

As the first evidence of what we "say" we believe...

And our faith-filled actions seal the deal and cause us to receive.

We receive salvation through faith...

Healing through faith...

Deliverance by faith.

We prophesy according to our faith.

We do all things according to and because of our faith.

If our faith is rooted in the faithfulness of God...

Then we know and are sure of this...

That He will never leave us or forsake us.

We must give our mind...will and emotions "over to Him"...

Or they will "take us away from" Him.

An un-sanctified imagination brings perverted revelation.

We must allow His Word to transform our mind

That we might have the mind of Christ.

Our will must be completely yielded to His will,
Or we will manipulate and control things...
In order to walk things out our own way.

Many people around you will want you
To move by "logic" and "reason,"
But we must move by the Spirit and revelation.
Many will try to talk you out of believing
That God speaks today...but keep listening anyway.
You only stand before God on the final day.
Then...they won't have much to say.

Our emotions must be dealt with...
Or we will continue to "react" instead of "respond."
The likeness and image of Jesus
Is continually being birthed and born in our lives...
By the yielding of our will to His will
And by the giving over of our flesh and feelings
To the Spirit of God.

Reactors...blow up and hurt people. Responders show up and heal people.

Isaiah 41:10, NKJV
> Fear not, for I am with you;
> Be not dismayed, for I am your God.

I will strengthen you, yes I will help you,
I will uphold you with My righteous right hand.

We have nothing...nothing...nothing...to fear...
When we keep HIM near.

Sometimes our days seem so busy...
Filled with more than we can do.
And our road seems rough and rugged...
And the mountains...insurmountable too.

Remember, the mountains of life
Are never as steep as they seem.
With faith in our heart...and a pep in our step,
We can accomplish our dream.

For nothing with God is impossible.
With..HIM...we will always achieve.
Have the courage to step out and do it.
You...have the faith to receive.

Faith is much greater than knowledge.
It has more power...than talents or skill.
Defeat will turn into triumph...
When we trust in God's wisdom and will.

By faith...we can move the mountains.
For there is nothing that God cannot do.
All we need is faith in our heart...
To believe that the dream will come true.

O, we may all have struggles.
But we do not have to fall.
We have His strength...in our weakness...
So, by faith...we can always stand tall.

And as we walk in obedience,
With confidence "in Him"...
We can trust that He will keep us...
When we are "out there on a limb."

Out beyond the limits,
Out...of our comfort zone...
Our faith is activated at those times...
When we walk in the unknown.

Trusting that HE knows the way,
And HE will bring us through.
Having faith that God alone...
Can DO what we cannot do.

So, Lord, I pray...in me fulfill
All the fullness of Your will.
In my life...and even in death,
In every moment...every breath.

My hope and joy...is in Your Son
So let Your will in me...be done!

The Faith of Mary

Luke 1:30-34, NIV

> But the angel said to her, "Do not be afraid, Mary; you have found favor with God. You will conceive and give birth to a son, and you are to call him Jesus. He will be great and will be called the Son of the Most High. The Lord God will give him the throne of his father David, and he will reign over Jacob's descendants forever; his kingdom will never end."
>
> "How will this be," Mary asked the angel, "since I am a virgin?"

I know what it means to "ponder."

It means to think about something carefully in your head,
To weigh it in your mind.
It implies a serious process of mental activity
And careful consideration of all the factors involved.

But what does it mean to "ponder something in your heart?"

The original Greek text uses both the word
That we translate into "ponder" and the word for "heart"
In the same sentence.

"Ponder," in the Greek, suggests not just considering
But also trying to put things together.

Doing it "in the heart" gives an important emotional overlay
To the process.
To ponder in our heart is to try to feel it out.
As well as to think it out.
Mary did not take what was happening to her
Just at face value;
She sought the deeper,
Divine intentions behind her experience.

She was perplexed and pondered what sort of greeting
The angel Gabriel gave her when he said,
"Greetings, favoured one! The Lord is with you" (Luke 1:28).

What makes Mary a model of faith
Is not only her willing submission to God's will,
But her struggle with that will for her life.

Mary, with her questions and ponderings,
Shows us the way to live in God's will...

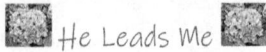

As we also ponder what God is doing
In our lives and world.

Mary's life was not easy
After her encounter with the angel,
And there were doubtless many more times
For questions and chances to ponder.
But, in the encounter with God...
Mary, like all of us who respond to Him with struggles,
Questions and ponderings, found favour and blessings.

Long ago, God had a plan.
When peace on Earth was rare...
He chose a girl...we call blessed.
She was pure...beyond compare.

Mary was this young girl's name.
Betrothed...but untouched by man...
She met an angel face to face.
And he revealed God's plan.

"Mary, you've received God's favour.
The Lord's plan...it will be done.
You shall conceive and then embrace...
God the Father's only Son.

"He shall be the King of Kings...
Emmanuel...God in the flesh.
Mary, He has chosen you.
You are favoured and highly blessed."

How could she understand this...
So great a mystery...
That she would carry the Son of God?
And the world's Saviour...He would be.

The breath of Heaven...was released.
In her innocence, she received...
The fullness of earth's redemption,
Because Mary said Yes...and believed.

What would the village...say about her?
Would her parents...send her away?
What would happen with Joseph?
The price...seemed too high to pay.

Mary pondered this precious thing...
In her prayers and in her heart.
She trusted Holy Spirit...
That Heaven would impart.

She didn't have to do it.
It was her choice...if she'd believe.
So she abandoned herself to the will of God...
And, by faith, she did receive.

She responded in trust and obedience...
Her courage tenacious and great.
As the Spirit visited upon her...
She walked out His plan and her fate.

She said, "Let it be, Lord...
According to Your plan...
That a deliverer would be born
To redeem sinful man."

She yielded her will...
In silent prayer...
Overwhelmed by the greatness...
Of the Child she'd bear.

Saying, "Let it be done, Lord...
ALL...You desire and say.
And I'll wrap a present...
To the world Christmas Day."

Faithful in Giving

God reminded me that everything in my life...
Should be seed that I am willing to sow...
Into the Kingdom of God...
That it might bear much fruit...
Bringing forth a harvest of souls.

Prosperity is NOT just about finances.
It "includes" finances,
But the Word of God says that "as [our] SOUL prospers"
So shall we prosper in ALL things...
And be in good health.
God delights in the prosperity of His children.

1 John 3:18, KJV

> My little children, let us not love in word, neither in tongue;
> but in deed and in truth.

God "so loved." He "so loved"...that He GAVE. Love was His motivation for giving.

Then Jesus...because of love...
For His Father and for us..."gave" His life...
To fulfill the mandate of God.
HE became the offering...the divine seed sown
And He became the first fruits of many...
Who would come to believe.

As we are faithful to put "action" to our love
And, in faith, we practice the "deed of sowing seed,"
We will also further advance the plan of the Kingdom,
And we will facilitate the purposes and plans of God...TODAY.

"Everything" in our life...should be "seed"
That we are willing to sow into the Kingdom of God
That it might bear much fruit...
And bring forth a harvest of souls.

Our time...energy...talents...gifts and finances...
As we give them to Him...
He will multiply them back to us.
Investing our time and making time available
To spend with the Lord pays great dividends
And causes us to become more and more like Him...

We may never "find" time
In our hectic schedule and our overflowing day...

But we can "make a little time"
To hear what Jesus has to say.
You see, that's "our choice,"
What we will or will not do.
But I know Jesus wants to spend
Some time with me and you.

When we make time for Jesus
And we let Him have "first place"...
It's amazing how the rest of the day will multiply...
And pick up pace.
He'll extend the hours, and we'll get all things done...
When we're faithful to spend some time
Basking in the "Son."

He will show us His purpose...
And share with us His plan...
When we seek His face and not just His hand.

He has a strategy. He has a way.
And He will share it with us...
As we make time in our day.
Waiting on the Lord is an investment, you see.
Spending time with Him...benefits you and me.

He says, "I have put you in an appointed place...
And I have given you My empowering grace.
Here, I can cause you to stretch and grow...
And here, there's mystery that I want you to know...
That the seed is within...
That which I have given you.
Open up the ears of your understanding
And you will know what I want you to do.

I have given seed to the sower...
And, as you are faithful to sow,
I'll be faithful to ensure
That what you've given...will grow.
Give out of your love...
And know My Word is true.
Receiving was My idea.
It will come back multiplied to you.

Be faithful in your giving...
For the day will come and you will see...
When buying and selling and trading...
Will no longer be.

But because you have been faithful...
My principles to keep...
Your supply will be established.
What you have sown...you shall reap.

I shall pour out over my children...
Increase and prosperity.
And ALL those still in darkness
Will "know" YOU "belong" to ME."

We are entering into a season of release and increase.
God wants us to live out of the overflow...
And have more than enough to "give"
Into "every good work."
Today, more than ever,
We need to reach out to the precious fruit of the earth
And the treasures hidden in the darkness.

The Lord kept saying to me,
"God WILL NOT BE MOCKED...
For 'whatever' a man sows...
SO SHALL he reap!
This is a sowing season...
And the harvest is great and plentiful," says the Lord!

Give and It Shall Be Given

Luke 6:38, NIV

> Give, and it will be given to you. A good measure, pressed down, shaken together and running over, will be poured into your lap. For with the measure you use, it will be measured to you

Give and it shall be given...
Pressed down, shaken together, and overflowing.
For great shall be the harvest
On the seed that you are sowing.

For this is the season of increase and abundance.
As you are obedient and follow My lead...
I will open the windows of Heaven
And supply for all your needs.

A season of picking up the pace...
Where you'll surpass your present place.
When you press into giving...
Through the power of My grace.

A time for offering the fullness of your life...
And making a difference wherever you go.
A time for pouring out My love...
As My goodness you continue to show.

My principles and My purpose...
Are in My Word...for all to see.
When you're faithful in your giving...
You can always trust in Me.

To multiply the blessings,
According to what I say...
My principles always work...
When you walk in My way.

There will be nothing lacking.
Your faithful giving will never be ignored.
There is absolutely nothing...
My riches in glory cannot afford.

As you are steadfast in your sowing...
Your field will yield much more.
It has never been My plan...
For My people to be poor.

But you are blessed to be a blessing.
That is my desire for My Bride.
So, rise up in your giving.
Your faith will never be denied.

There is a testing of your trust...
As you continue to sow your seed.
Sow according to My Word...
And according to My lead.

And your land shall be full...
Overflowing...yielding much grain.
As I pour out My abundance...
Time and time again.

As you deposit into your heavenly account...
Earthly withdrawals are on the way.
For the season of increase is upon you...
And My dividends...really pay!

Growing in Grace

Psalm 1:2-3, NKJV

> But his delight is in the law of the LORD.
> And in His law he meditates day and night.
> He shall be like a tree planted by the rivers of water,
> That brings forth its fruit in its season,
> Whose leaf also shall not wither
> And whatever he does shall prosper.

What a promise! Throughout our lives
As we stay planted in Him...
Attached to the Vine of life...
His supernatural, life-giving sap flows through to us
And we bear fruit.
We will not wither
And whatever we do shall prosper.

I'm my life, I've had much pleasure...
And I've also endured some pain.
I've laughed in the sunshine...

And I've cried in the rain.
I have been loved and left behind...
And I've been willing to try again.
I have suffered loss...and been alone.
And I have celebrated gain.

I've enjoyed the days of childhood...
Playing on slides and swings...
Carefree...without control...
Where life and laughter rings.

I survived the season called thirteen...
With all it's struggles and strife...
Working through insecurities...
While hating this time of my life.

All my teen years were a struggle...
With pressure from my peers.
Every day was full of drama...
And every night with tears.

I was coming to terms with who I was...
And who I was going to be.
And I began to realize...
The choice was up to me.

As a young adult, I flourished.
In business...I found my place.
I loved the tests and the trials...
The excitement and the pace.

The joy of being a new mommy...
Love fulfilled...and a heart at peace...
Caring for my little ones...
Brought such a sweet release.

The quest...to see them grow up...
Unscathed by the world so dark...
Brought struggles that left me sometimes weak...
And heartaches that left their mark.

But...it all served to better me...
The seasons of my life...
The pain and privilege of being a mother...
The pain and pleasure of being a wife.

Then the bittersweet days of ministry...
Full of potential...promise and plans...
Learning to walk by faith...
While putting all of it in God's hands.

Learning to trust that, no matter what...,
God is ultimately...on the throne.
Through the days of struggle and heartache...
And seasons of feeling alone.

Bearing the burden for others...
And learning to let it go.
Believing that God has the answer...
To things...that I just don't know.

Learning that people aren't perfect...
Learning to love and forgive...
Realizing that walking with Jesus...
Gave true purpose to the life that I live.

Mastering how to be selfless...
While putting others ahead of me.
Becoming a woman of grace...
And the very best I could be.

A life well lived is a precious gift...
Of hope...and strength and grace.
It's like a beautiful garment...
Of lavender and lace.

It has a lasting fragrance...
This legacy of pride and pleasure...
A loving.. lingering memory...
That we will forever treasure.

Life is happy, and life is sad...
Filled with smiles and tears.
Family...friends..good and bad times...
Year after year after year.

All things have worked together...
For my betterment and my good.
His Word has chartered the course of my days...
Just the way He said it would.

I thank God for this amazing life...
And for His unfolding plan.
My identity is found in Him...
And my life is in His hand.

God IS Love

1 John 4:7-12, NIV

Dear friends, let us love one another, for love comes from God. Everyone who loves has been born of God and knows God. Whoever does not love does not know God, because God is love. This is how God showed his love among us: He sent his one and only Son into the world that we might live through him. This is love: not that we have loved God, but that he loved us and sent his Son as an atoning sacrifice for our sins. Dear friends, since God so loved us, we also ought to love one another. No one has ever seen God; but if we love one another, God lives in us and his love is made complete in us.

God does not simply "love;"
HE is love itself.
Love is not merely one of His attributes;
It is His very nature.

The Scriptures say, "And we have come to know

And to believe the love that God has for us. God is love,
And the one who remains in love remains in God, and
God remains in him" (1 John 4:16).

Saying God is love is not to imply that love is God.
"God is love" means that God wants the very best for us.
God has our best interest in mind.
He wants to give us good gifts
And provide us with "all his benefits" (Psalm 103:2).

God is love. And He loves us all
No matter where we are in life.
God's love is unconditional.
God's love is without limit.
God loves us so much, and His love is so deep
That nothing can change His love or stop Him from loving us.

God loves us in every season of life.
He loves us every second of every day.
God's love is permanent.
It never fades, and He never takes it away.

God's love touches every part of our life.
Nothing...no calling or circumstance,
No adversity or advancement,
No pain or promotion,

No status or station in life
Escapes the brush strokes of God's love.
His love bleeds into the fabric and fibre of our lives.

God's love is amazing.
He knows everything about us and still loves us.
God knew that we were sinners,
Yet He forgave us and died in our place.
When we are sick, He heals.
If we fall off track...He pulls us back.
We deserved judgement, yet He gave us mercy.

When we put our faith in Jesus,
We find the Way...the Truth..the Life.
He's our Saviour and deliverer...
Offering hope in times of strife.

When the burdens seem too heavy..
And life is difficult and hard...
In Him...there's help and comfort.
"His love" is always our safeguard.

"His love" was always with us...
Before He even made the earth.
In our mother's womb, He formed our parts...
Giving us "identity and worth."

"His Love"...it cannot be described...
In simple shape...or form.
"His Love" is not an object.
"His Love" does not conform.

"His love" is uncontainable.
It spills out and overflows.
"His love" is unstoppable...
Wherever it ebbs and goes.

"His love" is unexplainable.
It's in spite of what He sees.
"His love" is unconditional...
Both in justice and mercy.

"His love" knew that we would stumble...
And sometimes suffer loss.
"His love" knew that we would choose to rise...
And follow Jesus...with "our cross."

"His love" always carries us.
"His love" holds us when we pray.
"His love" is the air we breathe...
And the fragrance of our day.

"His love" is ever enduring.
"His love" fully relieves.
As my mind is lost in thoughts of Him...
It is open...and receives.

"His love" brings me peace.
"His love" casts out fear.
"His love" melts my heart.
"His love" draws me near.

May we always know "His love"...
And that we are not alone.
So when the darkness comes...
We don't face it on our own.

When we need a loyal friend...
"His love" listens to our cares.
"His love" has the answers...
To our questions and our prayers.

"His love" knows what we need...
Before any words we say.
Nothing surprises Him...
When we call on Him and pray.

"His love" will always heal us...
As we let go of past harms.
"His love" will be our remedy...
As we are embraced within His arms.

"His love" will always forgive us...
When "we confess"... our sin.
He longs for us to open our heart...
And let "His love" fully in.

Godly Success

God designed us...for success.
He made us to be winners.
This is true for every person,
Regardless of what has happened in the past.
God has destined everyone to live the life abundant.

Jeremiah 29:11, NKJV

> For I know the thoughts that I think toward you, says the
> Lord, thoughts of peace, and not of evil, to give you a future
> and a hope.

God wants us to do what He has called us to do,
And He wants us to do it out of His ability.
Burnout happens when we operate
Out of our own strength and power.
God's never had one qualified person working for Him yet.
He equips those He calls.
When we will trust in the Lord and walk with Him,
We will accomplish day-by-day

The things He's planned for us.
And we will walk out the successful future...
He's already put in place.

The secret to a glorious life...is not a secret.
To me and you...success lies
In the everyday...things we say and do.

Talking every day with Jesus...
And walking with Him along the way...
Giving Him our heart and life...
As we trust Him and obey.

Sometimes...life is difficult...
And the road is rough and long.
But HE is always with us...
To fill our heart with song.

When friends and family hurt us...
In this life we live...
We can respond in love...
Say a prayer and forgive.

Jesus is our Everything...
In Him...our life's complete.
Jesus is our All-in-All.
He's our Refuge and Retreat.

With His peace...we will be comforted.
It soothes us...like a healing balm.
When we press into Jesus...
We're surrounded by His calm.

As we let His thoughts...lead us...
To a quiet...restful place...
We will meet each tomorrow...
With a smile on our face.

We will reach the goal we aim for...
And our dreams will all come true...
When we walk in plan and purpose...
The way God called us to...

May we always have a grateful heart.
Let us be thankful and satisfied.
Even when we're weary...
We know God is on our side.

Through this "life adventure"...
We are in His "constant care."
Of this truth...we are assured.
He is always there.

Success is not...a life that's easy.
There will be pain and sorrow.
But we will always overcome...
For He holds each "tomorrow."

Success comes through faith and trusting...
That HE will bear the load...
As we walk and talk with Jesus...
Along life's ever-changing road.

God's Shalom

As God's children, we can walk and live
In His true prosperity...His blessing ...favour and "shalom"...
The peace that Jesus won for us on the cross...
The complete...whole kind of peace...
Soundness...and overall welfare...
In the emotional...mental and physical realm.

His Shalom is perfect...in His relationship with us...
And in our relationships with others.

God's thoughts concerning our peace and prosperity
Are much deeper than we can perceive.
We are mistaken when our focus is on "finances" alone.
God's prosperity is complete and perfect...
His desire is to bless...to protect...
And to give us His grace and favour.
"Grace " and "favour"...that continually bring joy
And good will...benefit..bounty and rewards...
In the midst of whatever trial and test life affords.

His "shalom"...His peace...and joy...
His "prosperity" is a sustaining power
That carries us through everything.
Happiness is based on "happenings"
But joy is sustained through His Spirit...
No matter what happens!

When God shines His favour on me and you...
We have His love...His grace and His protection too.

Though we will still have trials...
His promises...are more.
Opportunities and promotion...
Will knock at our door.

We will have comfort...
And rest in His peace.
Our faith will have wings...
And our trust will not cease.

His hand...it will guide us...
In all that we do.
No matter what happens...
He will bring us through.

His blessings and mercies are new every day...
Even when things aren't going our way.
In the midst of the struggle...beauty is seen...
When on His understanding we trust and we lean.

When we seek first His Kingdom...
Through adversity...
All that we need will be ours.
That's prosperity!

When it's His face...we look to and pursue...
It will not matter the things we go through.

Joy and sorrow...smiles and tears...
Each day we share and trade.
Sometimes we walk in sunshine...
And other times in shade.

But keeping our eyes...on things above...
Will cause us not to forget His love.
When HE is our portion and our treasure...
We have true wealth...beyond measure.

Though storms may rage, and winds may blow...
And raging waters swell...
We can put our hand in His...
And trust that ALL is well.

For as our soul...does prosper...
So shall we prosper in ALL things.
Through ups and downs and thick and thin...
Whatever life may bring.

Hand in hand with Jesus...
Knowing HE will meet our needs...
Trusting and obeying...
And allowing Him to lead...
THAT'S TRUE PROSPERITY!

Proverbs 11:25, NIV

A generous person will prosper;
whoever refreshes others will be refreshed.

3 John 1:2, KJV

Beloved, I wish above all things that thou mayest prosper in
and be in health, even as thy soul prospereth.

God's Treasure

Jeremiah 1:2-8, NIV

> The word of the Lord came to him in the thirteenth year of the reign of Josiah son of Amon king of Judah, and through the reign of Jehoiakim son of Josiah king of Judah, down to the fifth month of the eleventh year of Zedekiah son of Josiah king of Judah, when the people of Jerusalem went into exile. The word of the Lord came to me, saying:
>
> "Before I formed you in the womb I knew you,
>   before you were born I set you apart;
>   I appointed you as a prophet to the nations."

WOW!

Psalm 139:13-16, NIV

> For you created my inmost being;
>   you knit me together in my mother's womb.
> I praise you because I am fearfully and wonderfully made;
>   your works are wonderful,

I know that full well.
My frame was not hidden from you
when I was made in the secret place,
when I was woven together in the depths of the earth.
Your eyes saw my unformed body

What a beautiful picture those words paint.
God knit us together in our mother's womb.
What a loving Father giving such intricate,
Creative attention to fashioning us...
Like the detail of a seamstress...
As she creates a beautiful garment one thread at a time.

"We have been remarkably and wonderfully made."

When God made you and me
He threw away the mold.
We are totally unique...
A one-of-a-kind creation,
Fashioned with awe-inspiring skill
By our loving and gracious Father...
From the top of our head right to the tip of our toes...
With a totally personal DNA and fingerprints.
We truly are..."fearfully and wonderfully" made!

The next time we look in the mirror...
Let's not look down on ourselves
Or compare ourselves to others,
Taking our cues from what the world says and sees.
But let's see ourself the way our Father...
The incredible Artisan who made us for Himself,
Sees us, in the fullness of our value and worth.

There is no one else in history like you and me.
He gave us a special personality...innate abilities...
Talents and spiritual gifts...
And then He applied the icing called plans and purpose
That set us apart for Him.

We are His beloved and cherished children...
Treasured creations...made in His very likeness and image.
God loves us...knows us...and yet wants us in every way.
He is ALL about us...
And desires that we would be ALL about Him.
We are God's treasure...
A gift to the earth.
And through all of our lives...
May we see His matchless worth.

He gave us the fruit of kindness.
He made us loving and giving.
He filled us with His Spirit...
To excel in our living.

We are His treasure...
Formed in royalty and style.
We are made in His likeness.
He went the extra mile.

He gave us a sound mind.
He gave us love and power.
We were made for "a time like this"...
Fashioned for this very hour.

He is the joy and the peace.
He is the love we bring.
He's given us wisdom in words...
And a heart unafraid to sing.

Our hands are always willing
To help others who are in need...
Being quick to reach out...
To pray and to clothe and to feed.

Yes...we are all God's treasures.
Let's share His goodness and grace...
And, through the power of His Spirit...
Transformation will take place.

Have Faith

Hebrews 11:6, NIV

And without faith it is impossible to please God, because anyone who comes to him must believe that he exists and that he rewards those who earnestly seek him.

As we have faith in what is not seen...
God rewards us for our belief in Him...
When we didn't need to SEE...to believe.

In order to see through the eyes of faith...
We have to close the mouth of reason.
We must never lose faith in "what we do know"
Because of what we don't know.
What finite mind can fully understand an infinite God?
He is more than we can ever comprehend...
And He is able to do exceedingly...abundantly more...
Than we could ever ask or think or imagine.
Who are "we" to put limits on a limitless God?
So many preachers today

Disqualify the "supernatural" power of God.
But HE IS THE "SAME...yesterday...today and forever."

We need help to mis-interpret that.
He is all powerful...all knowing...and always present.
We are His disciples...
And we are called to walk out "His ministry" in the earth today!

Today, if we preach the Word of God
And believe for signs following...
Just as the Word tells us to...
We are labeled a fanatic...or hyper-spiritual...or deceived.
The "religious" call us radical...extremists...even a cult.

Obviously...we don't have to try to be controversial.
Just preaching and walking in the truth...
Is controversial enough!

Preach the truth.
If we don't change the message...
The message changes us.

Faith is a persuasion...
The thing that "we believe"...
A steadfastly-set conviction...
From which we will not leave.
First...we must hear the Word

And believe that it is true.
And we will see how quickly
Faith...will come to me and you.

The Word of God is steadfast.
It will never change.
Every broken life...
It will remake and re-arrange.

It has the supernatural power...
To cause all things to be.
It's the blueprint for success...
When it's applied to ME.

Let's believe the Word is true...
In its totality...Old and New.
Don't think, because of Jesus,
The Old does not apply to you.

For we need the "full counsel"
Of His Word and plan.
Then we will take and possess
Our personal Promised Land.

Faith is founded "in truth," not in facts.
Facts change...but truth remains the same.

Success is not so much what we have "become,"
But what we have overcome.

He Is Our Champion

We can run our race...
Until our breath is gone.
Then Jesus, our Champion,
Gives us strength to carry on.

He will fight our battles...
When we feel we can no longer go.
He's the Champion of our faith...
And He causes it to grow.

At times, the ring of life gets lonely,
And we feel we're at a loss.
But we are overcomers.
He won the battle at the cross.

At times, we feel we'll never make it.
On the ropes we sometimes stumble.
God, our Champion and Deliverer,
Is helping keep us humble.

We cannot win this fight alone.
We need Him always on our team.
He knows the end from the beginning...
And what's happening behind the scenes.

He will cause us to stick with it.
His power will pull us through.
We will rise above it all...
Because of the Champion in me and you.

When we're in the ring with Jesus...
We are winners, you and me.
It's not only an extra one.
But, thank God, we have all three!

The Heart of a Child

Matthew 18:3, NIV

> Unless you change and become like little children, you will never enter the kingdom of heaven.

So let's wake up smiling
And receive the beautiful gift of being childlike
From our Father, the best father of all.

Give me the heart of a child...
Full of wonder to believe...
That everything belongs...
To the heart that just receives.

A child sees the wonders...
The earth...the sea and sky...
And his innocent heart knows...
That God's the reason why.

A child just believes...
To the very depth of their being.
They know that it will come...
Without ever seeing.

They know in their heart...
We'll do everything we say.
They have faith in us...
In their innocence each day.

We all get a little older...
And leave the days of youth.
Then we struggle and stumble...
With walking in the truth.

We listen to many teachers.
We dissect and analyze.
Our faith becomes diminished...
And unrest and doubts arise.

But our Father keeps on loving us.
He speaks in many ways...
In the breeze and through the storm...
Bearing with us every day.

Wooing us, "Come back...
To simple faithful ways...
Where you knew and trusted
That I was with you every day.

"Let the sunshine fill your heart.
Let your joy be full...not hiding.
Always do you part.
Let My love do the guiding.

"You'll soar to highest places...
In My time and for My reason.
Your purpose will grow wings...
In My appointed day and season.

"Just maintain your childlike faith.
Stand faithful and believe.
And you can trust Me to do my part...
As you stay ready to receive."

Heaven's Hope Chest

Matthew 6:19-21, KJV

> Lay not up for yourselves treasures upon earth, where moth and rust doth corrupt, and where thieves break through and steal: but lay up for yourselves treasures in heaven, where neither moth nor rust doth corrupt, and where thieves do not break through nor steal: for where your treasure is, there will your heart be also.

Open...Heaven's hope chest.
Come...and look inside.
See all the special treasures...
Stored up for you, my Bride.

I long to adorn you...
With jewels of every hue.
Come, open up My coffers...
And I'll pour out over you.

Heavenly solutions...
And answers to all you need...
Are within My special hope chest.
It's filled with every fruit-bearing seed.

I am always with you...
Right here by your side.
And I am pouring out Heaven's riches...
As I prepare and beautify My Bride.

There's supernatural provision...
And miracles in My hand.
I am leading you, beloved...
Into the Promised Land.

Come, open up My love chest.
Find your hope in Me.
It will all turn out the way...
I planned that...it would be.

Rise up and walk in truth.
Make yourself ready for Me.
I will produce the promise.
And cause your eyes to see.

That day is soon appearing...
When I will come for you, My Bride.
And I will find you worthy...
Having been tested and tried.

In the fires of adversity...
And the furnace of My grace...
You will stand transparent...
Reflecting Heaven's face.

Prepared and ready...
For our "special day"...
My beloved...
It's time to come away..

As you come away...
To My secret place...
All things will be accessible...
Through the fullness of My grace.

I so desire for My Bride...to be blessed.
Come away, beloved, and open Heaven's hope chest.

Hello, God

Psalm 34:17-19, ESV

> When the righteous cry for help, the Lord hears
>> and delivers them out of all their troubles.
> The Lord is near to the brokenhearted
>> and saves the crushed in spirit.
> Many are the afflictions of the righteous,
>> but the Lord delivers him out of them all.

Hello, God. Where are You?
We need to talk a while.
I mean, have You seen the bedlam...
Chaos, terror and trials?

At times I wonder if we'll make it.
We sure can't do it on our own.
Where are You, Lord? We need You.
We are feeling all alone.

There seems no way to keep...
Our nation safe and sound.
It's really past time God.
We need You to come and turn this place around.

Strengthen us in faith, Lord...
As we look on the horrors of the day,
And give us peace to accept the things...
We can't change in any way.
I'm trusting that You're listening...
And You're answering my plea.
You are working all things out.
You are not Absentee.

Lord, I know You always hear me.
You answer every time.
There's never a busy signal.
I've never had to pay a dime.

You are always reaching out.
You never stop working for our best.
You always care and You're involved...
So Your children will be blessed.

We know that You are with us, God...
In all the troubles and the sorrow.

Thanks for listening, God, today.
I will call again tomorrow.

Highway of Holiness

Romans 12:2, ESV

> Do not be conformed to this world, but be transformed by the renewal of your mind, that by testing you may discern what is the will of God, what is good and acceptable and perfect.

God uses circumstances to change us.
He wants the church to change.
He is giving us greater authority
As we press in to know the set times and seasons
Of His calendar...and as we walk by faith
Through the tests and trials of the times we are living in.

He is bringing a fresh revelation of the "highway of holiness"
And the narrow way...
That brings us through the transition to the new place...
The new way...the new life...in the Spirit.

Today, more than ever, we, as believers,
Need to make a fresh commitment to "follow" God...
To be "led by"His Spirit and to be "more like" Jesus!
We must lay down our lives once again
And take off the weight of those things
That so easily take us off track...
That we might be fully engaged
In the cause for Christ once again!

God is coming in a great way in this season.
He is about to visit us with a sweet fragrance
And strong demonstration of His Spirit.
He is going to release...increase...
To those who are actively doing "His works,"
And He will turn obstacles into stepping stones
As we continue to walk in "His ways."

Many are watching and listening to us,
Our actions...our words...our attitude,
As we come through the doors.
Paul said, "Follow me as I follow Christ."
May we be mindful of those who will follow after us...
And be good and faithful servants
Actively walking on the highway of holiness,
Helping others to possess their personal Promised Land.

Isaiah 35:8, NLT

> And a great road will go through that once deserted land.
>> It will be named the Highway of Holiness.
> Evil-minded people will never travel on it.
>> It will be only for those who walk in God's ways;
>> fools will never walk there.

The road to Heaven...is a "holy highway"...
Paved by the blood of God's Son.
It's the only road that arrives in Glory.
There is "no other one."

It's the narrow way...not the easy way.
There are tests and trials to face.
But He who fashioned the road we travel…
Imparts His strength and grace.

Many times we falter and fail...
And mistakes are made each day...
But as Children of God we're kept by His power…
On Heaven's Holy Highway...

We do not know what lies up ahead...
Or the troubles and trials we'll see.
But we know, whatever comes or unfolds,
The Lord walks with you and me.

This road...it will be difficult...
With obstacles to face...and overcome.
But we can walk through everything...
When we're walking with the "SON."

Rejoicing when there's sunny days...
Free from the storms of life...
And rejoicing in the growth that comes...
In the times of trouble and strife.

Whatever this road may bring to us...
Know it comes from the "Potter's hand."
And, as we allow the Lord to work in us...
We will fulfill His plan.

On this road, there's not much traffic...
For there are few who travel here.
Many are lost, exploring the interstates...
In vehicles called fear.

They're watching for the billboards...
Advertising pleasures that abound...
Choosing to take the exits...
Where sin and pleasures can be found.

Living in the fast lane...
Rushing to sins that loom and wait...
Concerned with living for the moment...
With no thought of eternal fate.

Everywhere there's temptation...
And it stares them in the eyes.
They don't look away.
Instead...they compromise.

How will they feel that dreadful day...
When from His throne...they hear Him say...
"I am the Way"...you did not take...
Though I appealed and pleaded...for your sake.

I am the Truth you did not heed.
You were so sure you had no need.
I am the Light...you "chose" not to see.
Now there's darkness...for eternity.

You cannot say, "I did not know."
I plainly spoke...and told you so.

At the end of this journey...they're guilty...
For they chose the wrong road to take.
Now pleasure is lost forever...
In a hot and fiery lake.

When the narrow way comes to an end...
We will find...our one "true Friend."
Christ's beautiful, wondrous and smiling face...
The place of acceptance...love and grace.

The road less travelled is the place to be.
It's the journey's end called destiny.
Here, before the "mercy seat." ...
The Lover of our souls we'll meet.

With His blood...He's covered our sin.
And we are invited...to come right in.

Matthew 7:13, NIV

> Enter through the narrow gate. For wide is the gate and
> broad is the road that leads to destruction, and many enter
> through it.

No matter how it "looks," God is "on the move,"
We are moving in the timetable of God Almighty,
And He WILL have His way.
When it's all said and done...and life's race is run,
It WILL be: "LORD, Your will be done!"

His Glory

Isaiah 37:16, NIV

> Lord Almighty, the God of Israel, enthroned between the
> cherubim, you alone are God over all the kingdoms of the
> earth. You have made heaven and earth.

Let it be filled with your glory!

In the Old Testament,
The children of Israel brought their riches of gold, silver,
And jewels into the wilderness tabernacle.
The tabernacle was filled with these symbols
To represent the glory of God.

When the Lord gave instruction for Solomon's temple,
He told them to overlay everything with gold,
Including the walls and ceiling.
Even the veil that separated the manifest glory of God
From the rest of the temple had golden thread woven into it.
God has always chosen to represent His glory...with gold.

The Word tells us that He will bring US forth as gold.
We are called to carry his presence here on Earth.
We are His temple.

If the glory of the Old Testament was just a fading glory
Then how much more does the Lord want to cover us
In the presence of His glory today?

I've thought about the simplicity of living
In the revelation of...and evidencing an open Heaven.
The Lord told me, "It's not difficult to live here,
And it's always open and available to My children."

He so longs for us to see
That His Glory is released as we walk...and talk...
And move and live..."in him."
We can move in His glory and have an open Heaven always...
The other realm is like the other room.

Romans 14:17, NIV

> For the kingdom of God is not a matter of eating and
> drinking, but of righteousness, peace and joy in the Holy
> Spirit.

Heaven...His glory is all around us.
And the Kingdom of Heaven is within us.

As we "move in it," we can impart it always...
And in "all ways."
It's everything we do and everything we say.
It's not about being "who we are."
It's about being "who He has caused us to be!"

I looked intently in the Spirit.
I saw Heaven opened wide.
I pressed in a little deeper...
For I longed to see inside.

I saw a company of angels.
They were everywhere.
They were singing and dancing...
Without a single care.

One of them looked at me...and said,
"Come on, step inside."
I wondered what had happened.
Was life over? Had I died?
They laughed...as they took hold of me, and said,
"No...you're here to get Heaven's precious treasures.
You're not walking fully in them yet.

"For you've desired the greater things...
To be manifested in the Earth.
So you must carry the person of God...

And know His matchless worth."
I looked...and I saw Patience...
With Love standing right beside.
There was Revelation and Understanding...
Of how to live and to abide.

I looked again, and there was Wisdom...
With a vessel full of faith.
I saw the Holy Spirit.
He was everyplace.

He had a golden horn of prayer.
And He began to pour it out,
Saying, "This will keep you strong...
And away from disbelief and doubt."

Peace and Joy were there...in plenty...
Praise and Worship...constant and clear.
I was overflowing with thanksgiving...
For the honour of being here.

I received strength and courage...
To help me run my race.
I wasn't ready yet to leave.
I needed more amazing grace.

I looked for Understanding...
Revelation...Boldness and Might...
To speak the truth of God's Word...
And be pleasing in His sight.

There were no words of judgment...
No accusation there...
No pain or loss or suffering...
None of those to bear.

God's personality...
Is Heaven's greatest treasure.
And He longs to pour it out in us...
Liberally and without measure.

Then I heard the Father's voice...
Ringing through the realms of eternity...
All of his attributes on display...
All given to you and me.

We...only have to choose them...
And allow God's life to be displayed.
They didn't cost us...a single thing.
The price was already paid.

Those who "know" their God...
Will do great and mighty things.
Faith will work by love.
And we'll move with supernatural wings.

And as we live..."in Him,"
All things will come to be.
In His character and image...
We'll live...supernaturally.

The Kingdom of Heaven's not hidden.
God says...It's not a mystery.
"It's ME moving in you...
And you moving in "ME."

His Peace

John 17:20, NIV

> My prayer is not for them alone. I pray also for those who
> will believe in me through their message.

This promise of peace extends to all of us
Who believe in Jesus' name and put our trust in Him.

When trouble and chaos surround me...
Your still waters ease my soul.
Into Your presence I retreat.
I'm at peace, and I'm made whole.

In the arms of Your Spirit...
The fires cannot burn.
I press into Your perfect peace...
For You alone I yearn.

I cannot fully grasp...
Nor can I comprehend.
Yet I know Your supernatural peace..
Is given without end.

It echoes through the darkness.
It's with me in solitude.
It comforts me and lifts me.
Out of every troubling mood.

It brings us an unexplainable calmness...
And a deep tranquillity.
We are bathed in His love and grace...
And eternal security.

There is a peace...
I can't explain.
It comes like a river...
When I call on His name.

"Let not your heart be troubled.
Neither let it be afraid..
For I have known you, and I've loved you...
Long before this world was made.

Peace I give and leave with you..
My peace I do impart..

As you seek Me and you find Me...
With the fullness of your heart.

Hold Fast to Confidence

Hebrews 10:35-36, NIV

> So do not throw away your confidence; it will be richly rewarded. You need to persevere so that when you have done the will of God, you will receive what he has promised.

Jesus gave us full forgiveness of sins..
And adopted us as sons and daughters,
And He transforms our hearts and our lives.

As a result, we have boldness and confidence
To enter the Most Holy Place
By a new and living way,
Into the very presence of God through Christ.

We have this incredible access and confidence.
And He tells us, "Don't throw that confidence away.
It belongs to you.
You have the grace to overcome and be empowered not to sin."
Our confidence is in Him.

It's based on the Word of God...
And the finished work of Jesus on the cross.

We can have God confidence,
Believing in His greatness...His strength, His integrity,
His sovereign power to do what needs to be done.

We can have full, complete confidence in God,
Confidence in the truth that God empowers us,
Engages us and strengthens us.

It is this confidence in God that makes it possible
To achieve and accomplish anything
And everything God sets before us.

In the moments I come to You, Lord,
When my faith wanes and is not strong,
You take me Into Your loving arms,
And tell me I belong.

You're there for me when I'm overwhelmed,
And I can't go any longer.
The confidence I have in you...
Every day grows stronger.

Because of Your grace and mercy
You're the living God we praise.
For Your manifold blessing and Your love,
Your name like an anthem we raise.

We lay our life down at Your feet.
Before Your throne we fall.
And by the power of Your Spirit,
You help us give to You our all.

You are my Strength, my Deliverer.
My gratitude won't go unspoken...
For the healing You have given...
To my heart, no longer broken.

I have confidence and courage...
When I let You lead the way.
I am convinced of Your care for me.
You assure me when I pray.

I can have such CONFIDENCE
In all Your loving ways...
Knowing You are with me...
As I walk in faith each day.

You didn't tell me life is easy,
But that You'd be here with me.
And that I could trust You always...
On calm or stormy seas.

All that we face today...
Prepares us for tomorrow.
Our faith will take our fear away.
And Your peace replaces sorrow.

You are the Lord of my life.
Nothing can ever steal that away.
Nothing can rob me of this truth,
Because, with me, You always stay.

You are my everything, Lord.
There is nothing the devil can do...
To shake my confidence and the faith...
That I have, dear Jesus, in you.

Hope: Past...Present...Future

Romans 8:24-25, NIV For in this hope we were saved. But hope that is seen is no hope at all. Who hopes for what they already have? But IF we hope for what we do not yet have, we wait for it patiently.

This is a "season of hope"...
The kind of hope that is A SURE EXPECTATION.
It takes hold of us and possesses us...
HOPE that is a confident expectation...
Based on the solid certainty of God's Word.
It rests in the truth of God's sure promises.
Let your "hope" be the groundwork of your faith.

"Today" is a gift from God...
And hope is found in this truth...
That "today"...no matter what happens...
No matter how hard the wind blows...
Or how nasty the storms of life rage...
Or if it seems like things are never going to change...

We "have hope" and we "know" that God is working
In us...for us...and through us to bring about the "best."
He will always turn for good what the devil meant for evil.

We are daily being refined by the fires of life.
They burn...but they also purify.
When we embrace them...we become stronger...
And our hope becomes SURE...
Being anchored in the unchanging truth
That He is always for us.
He's never going to leave us.
He is our everlasting Friend.
He's the Alpha and Omega, the Beginning and the End.

HE is our gift of hope: past...present and future!

Hope is faith's certainty.
Hope can endure...
When it's rooted in trust...
That is steadfast and sure.

Hope remains positive...
When the going gets tough.
Hope presses through faithfully...
Though things remain rough.

Hope continues to dream...
Of a better tomorrow.
Hope stands believing...
In the midst of the sorrow.

Hope is like a heavenly sound...
That guides our heart each day...
A melodious song of life and light...
That leads us in the way.

Hope is the voice in the dark of the night...
That quietly whispers, "It will all be all right"
Hope is the fire that burns in our heart.
Hope opens the way for faith to impart.

Hope shines and it sparkles...
Though there are tears in our eyes.
Hope is eternal.
Hope never dies.

Hope for the whole world...
The hopeless and lost...
Is the hope that was given...
That day on the cross.

Jesus is our Hope.
He is Heaven's precious Dove.
Hope now lives forever
Through His unchanging steadfast love.

So, when we feel discouraged...
Thinking no one really cares...
We have steadfast hope...in this:
God is always there.

When we place our hope...in HIM...
Our faith will soon be sight.
And we will walk in certainty...
In God's pure and revealing light.

Hebrews 6:19-20, ESV

We have this as a sure and steadfast anchor of the soul, a HOPE that enters into the inner place behind the curtain, where Jesus has tone as a forerunner, having become a high priest forever, in the order of Melchizedek.

Hope

Romans 15:13, NIV

> May the God of hope fill you with all joy and peace as you
> trust in him, so that by the power of the Holy Spirit you may
> abound in hope.

Hope is an essential ingredient for every believer.
It is that engine that keeps us going...
When everything else seems to be falling apart.

We are filled with hope when we accept Jesus.
As we continue on life's way, things happen...
Things change...
And we can feel downcast or abandoned and out of sorts.
If we lean into the Holy Spirit, we will find comfort
And renewed hope.

I know it's hard to hope for the best
When things look the worst.
It's difficult to look to the future

When everything seems to be so uncertain.
Having hope can get swallowed up...
In the multitude of words that are released...
Carrying a spirit of fear and death.

Thankfully, God's Word gives us the solution.

We can "have hope"
When we build our life on Jesus, the Solid Rock,
And if we plant our faith in Him,
We can trust that He'll take care of us.

Faith, hope and love are mighty forces
Meant to carry your life forward and upward.
They are not only our wings,
But the power to use them.

Hope plays a critical role in the exercising
Of our faith to believe.

It's pretty hard to hope
When natural circumstance cause us to be in fear and doubt.
It's difficult to love
When we've lost hope.
Hopelessness becomes...who cares?
What does it matter that we have faith if we have no hope?

Hope

Hope is the sunshine of life...the wind in our sails...
The spring in our step.
Hope is essential.
It's an anchor for our soul.

Having hope propels us to achieve our dreams...
And drives us forward toward our pursuits.
It keeps us afloat when everything seems to go wrong...
And when we feel like we're drowning.

Hope is the light at the end of the tunnel...
And the compass by which we navigate our lives...
Through trials and troubles toward our dreams.

When we lose hope, we are like a ship without a rudder...
Being tossed to and fro without direction.

Having hope keeps our boat afloat
And continuing to sail in the direction of our dream.

We can have hope...In our God.
He's all knowing.
From our lives, He's a river...of water,
Living and flowing.

He's a river of rest...
Giving hope and elation...
Flowing out from the well...
Of eternal salvation.

A life filled with hope...
Is the life that God planned.
He holds all of us...
In the palm of His hand.

When the storms come...
And there are trials to face...
When I can't find an answer...
I'll rest in His grace.

When life feels unfair...
And I've had all I can take...
I have hope in my Father.
He will never forsake.

God sees all of our struggles.
And in Him is our hope.
He has everything covered.
We don't need to cope.

Hope

With people and problems...
With stress and despair.
Just reach out in hope...
And He is right there.

I Choose

Philippians 3:12-14, NLT

> I don't mean to say that I have already achieved these things or that I have already reached perfection. But I press on to possess that perfection for which Christ Jesus first possessed me. No, dear brothers and sisters, I have not achieved it, but I focus on this one thing: Forgetting the past and looking forward to what lies ahead, I press on to reach the end of the race and receive the heavenly prize for which God, through Christ Jesus, is calling us.

This "ONE THING" I do. I "let go" of the past and press on
To "MY" future.

We make ourselves the "victim"
When we continually blame our past and other people
For our problems.
I was late for work because "they" wouldn't give me a ride...
I have no place to stay
Because they had too many rules for me to live by.

I wouldn't be this way if they had taken better care of me.
When I was a kid...My boss didn't see
How greatly "they" benefited because of ME.

WOW!

We think our "excuses" explain why...
Life hasn't worked out the way we would like.
We've been treated unfairly...got the short end of the stick...
Been dealt a lousy hand of cards.

After all, we are the victim of lousy circumstances...
And, because we accept and convince ourselves of this...
We go through life blaming other people
For the way "our" life is.

Most who are good at "making excuses"
Are really not good at anything else...
Because they have "excused" themselves
From having to be responsible...
By making "someone else" responsible for their failures.
They don't have any motivation to succeed...
Because, after all, it wasn't their fault they failed.
It's a vicious cycle...

Most of us "learn" from our mistakes
When we stop "defending" them.
We can give a lot of reasons
Why we can't do something.
What we need is ONE reason why we CAN!
The word can't is the enemy of success.

When we will embrace the truth
That "I CAN do ALL things through Christ
Who strengthens me"...
Then we will not make excuses
And continue to play the blame game.

The best years of my life began
When I trusted God for the future
And took ownership of my own life.
I stopped blaming my mom...my boss...my husband...
My friends...my circumstances...my situation...
And made a decision that "my destiny" was in "my hands."
Even God cannot fix my problems...if I am the problem!

God can bring destiny from disaster
When we make a decision to let go of what lies behind
And press forward to doing what God has called us to do.
Many make it harder than it needs to be...
Because they go back and forth...double minded...

Wavering between the world and the Kingdom...
Continuing to blame the old for keeping them from the new.
This ONE thing I DO. I "FORGET" what lies behind...
And press forward...no excuses...
Stop justifying WHY you are...the way you are.
Don't defend. Just amend.

The verse says press on to "make it my own."
Stop making it someone else's problem.
Stop making "our life" the responsibility of another.
We are all responsible for our choices...
And for the consequences of them.

Winners accept and deal with the shame.
Losers just make excuses and lay blame.

I choose...to win or lose.
It's always up to me.
I can rise to win the fight...
Or just a victim be.

I can live "My Life" each day...
Or, in regret, live an excuse.
I can live for God and others...
Or live like a recluse.

Always blaming someone else...
For the way "my life" turned out...
Never choosing to move by faith...
Because I can't...let go of doubt.

Always looking backward...
To the way things "used to be"...
Giving me a reason...
So...the problem...can't be ME.

Wanting to live "MY" life...
Without...responsibility...
So when anything goes wrong...
No one can blame me.

Things will never change...if we remain the same.
The winds of change are blowing. It's time!

I Will Worship

Daniel 3:16-18, NIV

Shadrach, Meshach and Abednego replied to him, "King Nebuchadnezzar, we do not need to defend ourselves before you in this matter. If we are thrown into the blazing furnace, the God we serve is able to deliver us from it, and he will deliver us from Your Majesty's hand. But even if he does not, we want you to know, Your Majesty, that we will not serve your gods or worship the image of gold you have set up."

When the fires of persecution and affliction come into our life...
We need to remember this truth:
God is using it to free us from some of the things...
That have had us bound...
And assure us of His constant commitment to us
To refine and purify us.

The flames burn away the strings of sins...
That attach themselves...bad attitudes and habits...
Wrong heart motives and intentions.

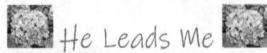

In the midst of the storms we are facing...
And any troubles we're traveling through...
Know we are not alone.
He's there and will comfort us in the midst of every situation
So we can comfort others.

2 Corinthians 1:10, MSG

> Instead of trusting in our own strength or wits to get out of it, we were forced to trust God totally not a bad idea since he's the God who raises the dead!

And rescued us he did and set us free from certain doom.
He will do it again and again...
Rescuing us as many times as we need rescuing.
When we will not bow to idols...to duties...
Delights and desires, but we continue to worship Him...
And live or die by the Word of God...
Upholding that standard in our lives.

Shadrach, Meshach and Abednego were not rude to the king.
They called him Your Majesty, but they made it clear...
That they would not bow down to an idol…
That they worshipped God alone.

Today we have to be respectful to those who are in leadership
But we cannot bow down to the world's way

And worship man.
We must be free to worship God.

I will worship in the morning.
I will praise You day and night.
I'm so thankful for salvation...
And for Your eternal light.

I'll worship in the storm.
I'll sing in trouble and the rain.
When problems pull and press...
I'll worship You again.

Though some may try to stop me...
And take away my right...
I will rise and worship...
And put the enemy to flight.

No matter what they say...
Or what they try to do...
I will walk in love.
And I will worship You.

I will worship You, my King.
And, with every word I say,
I will tell the story.
Of my new life...and Your way.

I will worship in the sunshine.
I'll praise You in the rain.
Lord, I will be faithful...
Through the healing and the pain.

You will forever be my Answer...
And my very great Reward.
I will never love another.
I will worship You, my Lord.

You are my loving Father.
You mean everything to me.
You've given life abundant...
And established my identity.

I will love and worship You forever.
You're my Refuge and High Tower.
I will believe You for all things...
Trusting in Your grace and power.

I will worship You, Lord!
You are my All-and-All.
I know, when I'm in need...
You always hear me when I call.

You are all I want.
You are all that I desire.
You have baptized me with love...
And Your Holy Spirit fire.

You purify me and sanctify me...
To rise and hear and do.
Through all the seasons of my life...
I will worship You.

Jesus Is

Psalm 117:2, NLT
> For his unfailing love for us is powerful;
>> the Lord's faithfulness endures forever.
> Praise the Lord!

Jesus, my Lord, inspires me.
So, I sing to praise His name.
He's the only one who is...truly worthy
Of all fame.

There is no other person.
And never will there be...
Anyone like Jesus...
The King of Eternity.

There's nothing as wonderful as Jesus...
Nothing as beautiful as His face...
Nothing as awesome as His power...
And nothing as amazing as His grace.

Nothing as unconditional...
As the love He has for you and me...
Nothing as strong and powerful.
And never will there be.
Nothing that shines so bright...
As His eternal glory.
And nothing has the impact...
As His astounding story.

I sing because ...I love Him.
I'm so grateful for all He's done.
Because He died and rose again...
The battle has been won.

All my days I'll praise Him...
For all He's done for me.
He bound up my broken heart...
And He set this captive free.

I live and love to tell His story,
My dearest Saviour...coming King.
He fills my life with gladness...
And my heart, with love it sings.

He means everything to me.
Of His greatness I will tell.

With Jesus Christ, we have it all.
Without Him...it's just Hell!

Jesus Knows

Romans 8:38-39, NIV

> For I am convinced that neither death nor life, neither angels nor demons, neither the present nor the future, nor any powers, neither height nor depth, nor anything else in all creation, will be able to separate us from the love of God that is in Christ Jesus our Lord.

Sin entered the world...
Because Adam and Eve rejected God and His command.
Then, in turn, they faced God's eternal rejection.
And we also were placed under a curse...
Of separation from His favour and bound to His wrath.

But Jesus redeemed us from that curse
And took it upon Himself.
He redeemed us. He chose us.
He bought us back and paid the price.
He accepted us in the beloved...
The very highest place of acceptance.

By the word of truth and the power of the Spirit
We have received the "Spirit of adoption" (see Romans 8:15).

How wonderful that this is a permanent, binding acceptance.
Nothing can separate us from the Father's love
(see Romans 8:38-39).
Man's rejection is made so small In light of the truth,
That through the Gospel, we have...
God's eternal love and acceptance...unconditionally.

Jesus knows our every hurt.
He understands our grief.
But through His love and grace...
Our heart will find relief.

He has suffered and known sorrow.
He's felt betrayal's spiteful sting.
Through the trials of our lives...
We are sheltered by His wings.

He's aware of all our deepest wounds.
He hears when others put us down.
His favour...forgiveness and mercy...
Will be our light and crown.

He identifies with rejection...
The way our heart does ache.
He brings healing and comfort...
To feelings hard to shake.

For He, too, was rejected...
His feelings disregarded...
He was beaten and abused...
His very life discarded.

Jesus knows our every pain...
And His faithfulness is sure.
In all that still concerns us...
Redemption brought the cure.

Jesus Paid It All

1 Peter 3:18, NIV

> For Christ also suffered once for sins, the righteous for the
> unrighteous, to bring you to God. He was put to death in
> the body but made alive in the Spirit.

Calvary's hill was a place of shame...
But, for our sakes, our Saviour came.
He gave Himself for you and me...
So we could live eternally.

When they stripped Him of His robe...
And threw Him to the ground...
He could have summoned all of Heaven's angels...
But He didn't make a sound.

And here, in this place of great mercy,
God's Son died...in sinful man's place.
He took our sins and shame upon Himself...
And covered us with grace.

The cross is a place of atonement.
His blood alone...is all we need.
Our sins are washed away forever...
By His faithful giving deed.

As the blood and water flowed...
Salvation's plan was executed and sealed.
And as we give our hearts to Him...
The wounds of sin are healed.

No earthly riches could pay that price.
The blood of Jesus...was the supreme sacrifice.
His righteousness...is to us applied.
When we trust and believe...we are justified.

We cannot "earn entrance" through Heaven's gate...
Not by our works...whether small or great.
His precious blood only...will turn the key...
To eternal life...for you and me.

The nails did not hold Him in that place.
It was God's love. It was His grace.
Loving us...in spite of all we'd done...
God sacrificed His only Son.

The flames of Hell...will never touch me.
For Jesus bore my sins...at Calvary.
I'll stand at the Judgment Seat secure.
Of His love and grace...I will be sure.

And when I come...before His throne...
I will stand complete in Him alone.
And at His feet...I will lay down...
All my heart and earthly crowns.

Remembering all He did for me...
When He gave His life on Calvary.

Let's carry the cross each day in our heart...
As a reminder to you and me...
That Jesus alone is Lord of our life...
If only...we let him be!

JESUS...paid it all!

Jesus, Take the Wheel

James 4:13-15, NIV

> Now listen, you who say, "Today or tomorrow we will go to this or that city, spend a year there, carry on business and make money." Why, you do not even know what will happen tomorrow. What is your life? You are a mist that appears for a little while and then vanishes. Instead, you ought to say, "IF it is the Lord's will, we will live and do this or that."

We are not in control.
It's arrogant, he says, to think we are.
God is in control.

Even in situations where we like to say...
God is permitting it...He is permitting it by design.
He has a purpose in all things.
When we permit something...in our kids' lives...
We allow it because we are in charge of them.
God permits because it fits into the overall pattern
Of what He is doing.

We can get so out of sorts...
When we have a problem to deal with.
God wasn't surprised.
He actually knew what things were headed our way,
And was already planning to help get us through them.

Psalm 139 tells us that God is familiar with all our ways—
Where we've been, what we're doing now,
And where we're going.
Be assured and convinced that God is in absolute control.

God is on our side, and He is worthy of our trust.
We can give Him full control of our lives.
Release the wheel.
He knows exactly what He is doing...and where we are going.

Jesus, take the wheel...
And lead me down life's road.
Let me know You're always here.
And help me bear my load.
At times, this road is bumpy...
And the stops to rest are few.
Sometimes I can get off road...
And I don't know what to do.
In places the road is narrow.
There seems no end in sight.

My journey seems so long and dark...
Deep into the night.

I look for signs...along the way...
But You do not reveal.
I seem to have steered off the course.
Please, Jesus, take the wheel.

Get me back to the place...
Where I hear You speak to me.
On the road to destiny...
Is where I want to be.

Drive me down the Holy Highway...
Through the winds and storms and rain.
Lord, take the wheel...
In my hurt...despair and pain.

You're given me a road map...
That will safely lead me home.
But I will never make it...
If I try it on my own.

When I give You the wheel..
Faith and strength I find.

The road I travel with You...
Gives me peace of heart and mind.

The road may be full of bends and curves...
From beginning to the end.
When Jesus has the wheel...
We travel with our dearest friend.

He may take us to a place or two...
That we don't understand.
But we can always trust...
In God's unchanging love and hand.

There may be a detour...
A road block or two.
But there will be no dead ends...
On the road He travels with me and you.

Jesus, take the wheel...
And help me bear my load.
And I'll sit in the passenger seat...
As You drive me down life's road.

The Joy of Motherhood

Deuteronomy 6:5-9, ESV

> You shall love the LORD your God with all your heart and with all your soul and with all your might. And these words that I command you today shall be on your heart. You shall teach them diligently to your children, and shall talk of them when you sit in your house, and when you walk by the way, and when you lie down, and when you rise. You shall bind them as a sign on your hand, and they shall be as frontlets between your eyes. You shall write them on the doorposts of your house and on your gates.

God created motherhood...
To be an incredibly powerful force...
And one of the linchpins of the family structure.
God created the female heart and life engine...
To have unlimited power to love nurture, shape...
And mold the lives of their children.

As we faithfully parent our children and make them a priority...

Not just a fulfillment of desire but a commitment...
Staying constant in their lives...
And showing them the love and grace of God...
Forgiving them...confronting them...
And "showing" them the way to live through our own lifestyle.
Motherhood has been the toughest job...I've ever LOVED!

The joy of being a mom...
Has afforded me many things.
At times, it's broken my heart.
And other times, it's made it sing.

It's brought me pride and joy...
And sometimes sadness and pain.
It taught me faith and strength...
And how to dance in the rain.

I experienced loving someone...
More than my heart could bear.
You were always on my mind...
And always in my prayer.

I know about unfailing love...
And how to be a guiding hand.
How faith and trust in God...
Empower a parent to stand.
My love...became patient.

My love...became kind.
At times, it was all-seeing.
And at times, it was blind.

My love cared for and protected.
Perseverance was a must...
Fighting against the enemy...
And "knowing" HIM...in whom I trust.

He would never fail me...
As I pressed into His perfect plan.
He walks through life beside me...
Heart to heart and hand in hand.

A mom's love is always honest...
Not lying and deceiving.
And when the darkness comes...
We keep right on believing.

My love for my kids...
It will never forsake.
It's the kind of love that gives...
Much more than it takes.

It's the love that stands for truth.
It's just, and it's fair...
Not always seeing eye to eye...
But always being there.

It's the love that confronts...
When it's the right thing to do...
Not always "loving behaviour"...
But always loving "you."

It's the love that Jesus taught me...
As I've walked through this life...
With sunny days and blue skies...
And heartache...loss and strife.

It's the love that never changes...
No matter the problem or reason.
It's the love that grows and blossoms...
In each and every season.

It's love that's never selfish...
Self-seeking or cruel.
It follows after the Father...
And obeys the Golden Rule.

Love never turns its back...
Or turns itself away.
Love is faithful and forbearing...
Each and every day.

There has been no greater blessing...
Or accomplishment done...
Than to be my awesome daughter's mother...
And raise a strong and wonderful son.

God made this mother's love enduring...
In all things...and come what may...
So that nothing can destroy it...
Or take this love away.

There is no deeper joy...
That I have ever known.
Though you belong first to God...
And are only mine...on loan.

A mom's love is something...
Always caring...always giving...
That even when she's gone...
In her children...she's still living.

When my parenting days are over...
And I'm standing in "the SON"...
I'm believing to hear my Father say,
"Well done. My faithful one!"

Laugh at the Future

Philippians 4:6-7, NIV

> Do not be anxious about anything, but in every situation, by prayer and petition, with thanksgiving, present your requests to God. And the peace of God, which transcends all understanding, will guard your hearts and your minds in Christ Jesus.

When we're looking to God, and trusting Him,
We are free from worry.
We are free from fear of the future.

None of us knows what's coming into our life tomorrow...
Or next week or next month or a year...from now...
But we could conjure up and worry about all kinds of things...
If we look at the world instead of keeping our focus on Jesus.

My hubby and I were discussing some unknowns
And the future...and it can cause worry and anxiety.
I said to him, "The more things that happen..

The more we are seeing that we just have to trust God.

We have no control over what's happening...

So we can't do anything but press into faith...

Knowing that the same God who did so many things in our life..

Has not stopped His loving involvement

In our day-to-day activities.

Of course, we are still human...

And we have feelings...and emotions to deal with.

Life is not always easy...the future is never guaranteed...

To go the way we think it should or want it to.

If we have the fear of God...and faith in His abilities

We can have the strength to face...

Whatever the future may bring.

God knows the end from the beginning.

He knows what the future holds.

And HE holds the future.

God help us...not to worry...or speculate...

Or meditate on wrong things.

Help us not to be anxious..and not always be looking ahead,

Trying to figure out what's going to happen.

Lord, let us receive Your peace that passes all understanding.
I pray over every person with me today
And reading right now,
Every woman and man...and over my own life.
Help us to laugh at the time to come,
To be dressed in strength and dignity...
And confidence, as we put our faith in You...
And continue to look to You...
And not the issues in the world.

Deliver us from fear of the future.
Help us to rest in the truth...
That You hold the future in Your hands...
And You hold us in Your hands too.

What does the future hold?
How will things turn out to be?
I can't be certain of anything...
But I am sure God holds me.

When the storms overwhelm us...
We can rest in God's grace.
He is the Solution...
To the trials we face.

When the future's uncertain...
And I cannot see...
I can look to my Father.
He's always with me.

He knows every struggle...
Every bend in the road...
Every heartache and burden...
Because He shares every load.

So, I can laugh at the future...
Whatever may be...
Because I trust my Father...
To take care of me.

Little Eyes

Isaiah 54:13, NKJV

> All your children shall be taught by the Lord,
> And great shall be the peace of your children.

As a mom today, maybe you're struggling with heartache.
Maybe your children are estranged...
Or you're going through a difficult struggle
With a son or a daughter who are lost to you
And caught up in drug addiction or alcoholism.

Many times, the rewards of motherhood are delayed...
As God works in the midst of the mess
To bring forth a miracle.
I myself waited ten years for my precious son to turn around
And come back home.

Our children will not automatically walk in the truth.
Children need prayer. They need example.
They need loving discipline and correction.

If we leave our kids on autopilot...
Playing games and always on their tablet
Or watching TV and "out of our hair"...
He or she will crash and burn.
We must get up and set the example ourselves.

We must walk in the truth...
If we hope for them to walk in the truth.
We must practice our faith and be constant in their lives...
To "show them," not just tell them.

Maybe you're saying today, "This is too little too late."
But God is saying, "I redeem the time...
And whatever you will give to Me today...
To change and realign...
I will multiply into the lives of your children.
We can't change what happened yesterday.
But, as moms today:

Let's know the truth so we can live the truth...
And, through us, our children and our grandchildren
Will see Him in us...
And be drawn to His love and forgiveness.

Lets continue in faith in our actions...

And in the way we walk in His peace...

And set a godly example for our grown children and grandkids.

There are little eyes...

Observing you night and day.

There are little ears that hear...

Every word you have to say.

Little hands all eager to help...

To do everything...you do.

A little one who's dreaming of...

The day he or she will be like you.

You are someone's hero.

So, let your attitude reflect...

Kindness...love and grace...

Teaching them to show respect.

They believe in you sincerely...

As they watch your life unfold.

They will say and do what they see...

Not what they are told.

There's an innocent little one...
Who believes you're always right.
You're the perfect mom or dad...
In their thoughts and in their sight.

You are setting an example...
Every day...in all you do.
For the little child who's waiting...
To grow up...and be like you.

Love Encounter

Psalm 59:16, ESV

> But I will sing of your strength;
>> I will sing aloud of your steadfast love in the morning...
> For you have been to me a fortress
>> and a refuge in the day of my distress.

We are all in a storm...
But we are not all in the same storm.

Some are alone, with not a single person around to see...
No one to talk with or share with or live with.

People who struggle with mental illness...
And don't really understand what is really going on.

Young people, alone in their first apartment...
Miles from family or friends...
That had dreams of finishing their education and graduating.

Some realize there's a storm, but they're safely tucked away
Riding it out, with no real worries on the other side of it.

Some are feeling the raging of the storm...
With the loss of their job...
And the concern of not being able to pay the rent or mortgage...
And struggling to put food on the table.

Some are without a car or any way to get what they need...
And have to rely on others to help them.

Let's press into the compassion of God in this season...
And learn to walk a mile in someone else's shoes.

Overflow in this place
Fill our hearts with Your love
Your love surrounds us
You're the reason we came
To "encounter" Your love
Your love surrounds us.[1]

And the Lord said:

Because of ME, you are a "love encounter"...
And I want others to encounter My love through you.

---

1. *Here As In Heaven* by Matthews Thabo Ntele, Steven Furtick and Wade Joye

He handed me a golden key, and He said,
"This is the key of humility...
And it will unlock the Kingdom for you and for others."

He said, "Many today are offended and operate in the pride
That thinks they're above being questioned...
Or disagreed with...
And they can do whatever they want."
But the Lord said, "I came NOT to do my own will...
But the will of the Father who sent me."

He said, "Offence builds 'a fence'
That keeps us from being a love encounter.
He desires that the fences would come down...
And we yield our emotions and behaviour...to Him.

Social media today love and encourage critical comments
Because criticism draws attention.

Catty comments...attract clever retorts...
Abusive language and disrespect.
Bad news far outsells good news.
And harsh and hurtful words, unfortunately, make headlines.

So many verbal assassins are free to shoot and kill others
With the vocal expressions of the fullness of their heart.

Beloveds, this should not be so.
No wonder God put us in time-out...
So we could have revival come to our "Christian attitude."

God takes no pleasure in our suffering through this season.
His desire for us, in the midst of the crisis we are experiencing,
Is that it will generate humility...
And cause us to recognize our own sins...
And change our own behaviour...
As we take the beam out of our own eye...
And stop looking at the speck in our brother's.

Yield yourself to Me.
Humility's the key.
It opens you up to intimacy...
And the "grace to overcome."

God wants us to humble ourselves...
And let go of any of our "me-only" ways...
And be a true "love encounter" to others.

Lord, help us be humble.
Turn us from our pride.
And, in Your sweet presence,
May we always abide.

Lord, show us where...
Our ego's become so big...
That we've taken the place...
That belongs to Your Son.

Humble us, Lord.
Meet us face to face...
In the place of Your glory...
Your goodness and grace.

Open our eyes...
To narcissist ways.
You alone God are worthy...
Of man's worship and praise.

Help us not to be offended...
With those You love.
Let grace and forgiveness...
Be like a hand in a glove.

Lord, humble our hearts...
So others will feel...
Your presence and power...
Alive and so real.

And when things are hard...
We'll obey "Your voice."
Your ways are much higher...
Than personal choice.

When others hurt us...
Talk badly and scheme...
Let us remember...
We are part of "Your team."

May we always be ready...
To do what You've called us to do...
Knowing ALL of our life...
Belongs only to You.

Love Is

John 13:34-35, NIV

A new command I give you: Love one another. As I have loved you, so you must love one another. 35 By this everyone will know that you are my disciples, if you love one another.

Love is an emotion...
Strong...steadfast and pure.
And love is a decision...
To stand loyal..and endure.

Love's a supernatural force...
Prevailing through...the highs and lows.
It can move the mountains...
Withstanding...all life's blows.

Love is "life's victory"...
A glorious goal attained...
The covenant of lives and hearts...
A union God Himself ordained.

Love is a champion...
Fighting till death do us part...
Upholding the standards of truth and peace...
Guarding and keeping our hearts.

Love is an emblem of forever...
Eternal and sincere...
A flame that burns without regret...
Outliving earthly years.

Love is what life's all about.
It's the mystery of the ages.
You can see it clearly in His Word...
Throughout all its pages.

His love will guide the wayward heart...
And cast light upon our way.
Love is willing and available...
Each and every day.

Love is...someone special...
On who you can depend...
To share your laughter and your tears...
A partner...and true friend.

Love is...sharing and caring...
Helping another's dream come true.
Love is unselfish...preferring...
Putting others ahead of you.

Love is a reality...
Not a daydream of the mind.
It is not an illusion...
Or impossible to find.

Love is a "Person"...
And when HE invades your being...
There comes a new perspective...
And a better way of "seeing."

No longer do we look at things...
Through the emotions and the soul.
We see things by His Spirit.
His response...becomes our goal.

The day that I met Jesus...
I began to see...
"That Love"...is tangible. It is real.
And it lives inside of me.

Make Me Ready

Philippians 1:6, NLT

> And I am certain that God, who began the good work within
> you, will continue his work until it is finally finished on the
> day when Christ Jesus returns.

Change and sanctification happen in the midst of habitation.
God puts us with people...in places and in circumstances...
That allow what's on the inside of us...
To be brought to the surface
So that we can see them and choose...
To yield back to the Holy Spirit...
The behaviours that are not pleasing.

We need divine grace to consistently lead a changed life.
Only God's grace empowers us to turn away from wrong actions.
The grace that saves us trains us to live our life for God.
God compels us through the indwelling of Holy Spirit...
And empowers us by His power to live changed lives.

Changing and becoming like Jesus is a lifelong process of renewal.
Day to day, as we continue to peer...
Into the mirror of process with Holy Spirit.
And, as we spend time with Jesus and in His Word...
We will see the difference between the old and the new...
You and me.
We may not yet be who we want to be
Or who we're going to be,
But we sure aren't like we used to be!

Lord, I am Your vessel.
May I be ready for You to use...
To reach out and touch others...
Or in any way You choose.

Help me press into Your purpose...
And yield to You my will...
That I will walk in love and grace...
Using all God-given skills.

I will be a vessel of honour...
Fit to carry Your glory.
My heart will forever praise You.
And my lips will share Your story.

As I yield to Your Spirit...
I will be empowered by You...
To say whatever You ask me...
And do all I'm called to do.

Through the power of Your Spirit...
I'll be made ready for You to use.
In any and every capacity...
That You, my Lord, may choose.

The Mother Heart of God

Make no mistake: Our Father in Heaven is our Father.
However, His maternal nature guarantees...
That every bird is fed.
He numbers the hair on billions of heads.
He has innumerable thoughts about us

He is with us in our storms, comforting us...
And bringing healing to our hearts...and our diseases,
And He lavishes us with forgiveness for all things.

Like a mother, He deliberately forgets...
His children's shortcomings, and sins...
And casts them as far as the east is from the west,
Until they sink to the floor of the Sea of Forgetfulness.

It's so amazing: God made man in His image,
Both male and female.
Adam was created complete. He was all one.
We read that as "alone,"
But he was originally created "all one."

Then God saw that it was not good...
For man to be all one...or alone...
So he put Adam into a deep sleep...
And created woman out of man...
And made a helpmate suitable for him...
That would complete him again.

We can feel a mother's heart beating through Father God...
Ready to wipe every tear...kiss every boo boo...
Stay with us through the night and listen to our troubles...
There to love us unconditionally...
Help us to change...help us to grow...
And be the very best we can be!

A mother's heart is for her children.
With tender love, her eyes do glow.
She's a constant inspiration.
There's not much she doesn't know.

She gives herself so freely.
She shares every aspect of her life.
She always loves her children.
Even when they cause her strife.

She's full of compassion.
Her voice is strong, yet sweet.

She reaches out to help...
Those living in the street.

She is a woman of virtue.
She stands out among the rest.
She looks after all her household...
And brings to them...her best.

A woman who will brave the storm...
Knowing she is not alone...
She keeps her focus on the Lord...
And trusts in the grace He's always shown.

Mom always sees our struggles...
And every bend that's in the road.
She's always there to help us...
Carry every load.

A ,other's love is special.
It's full of grace and prayer.
She is always watching over us.
And, like Father God, she's always there.

Patience

Philippians 4:6

> Do not be anxious about anything, but in everything by prayer and supplication with thanksgiving let your requests be made known to God.

We can lose our patience...
When we can't see the grace of God in the situation...
He has placed us into.
I have to believe, in faith, that God knows what He is doing. I have to believe that whatever the intended end is...
For this situation comes from a loving, merciful...
And compassionate God.
If I don't, I won't remain patient. I will lose my patience.

Will I get frustrated? Will I get angry at God?
Will I get critical about the people...
And the circumstances around me?
Will I just give up and miss out?

Imagine what would have happened if Job had given up.
Job did not see the end intended by God.
He did not understand, at the time,
That God was working good in the situation he was in.

Everyone around him told Job to "lose his patience."
But he didn't..and we have the power...
To press through, on the inside of you and me.
And we can draw on the Spirit for the fruit of patience...
To be borne on our living tree.

Patience is a fruit that is greater...
Than knowledge or power or skill.
When we understand that "in waiting"...
We are trusting alone in God's will.

It is in the waiting...
That we will know our fate.
He will still our anxious heart...
As we prayerfully...patiently wait.

God knows the end of a matter...
From its very start.
As we practice our patience...
He assures our mind and heart.

As we are patient and long-suffering...
Bearing with one another in grace...
We'll become more like Jesus.
And we'll reflect His face.

And patience will cause our faith to arise...
Till there's nothing that we can't achieve.
Patience and faith work together...
To bring forth the things we believe.

Press into the fullness of His Spirit...
The promise of unending grace.
Press into dunamis power...
That brings transformation to this place.

Peace-Loving

James 1:2, NASB

> Consider it all joy, my brethren, when you encounter various trials.

A "peace-loving" person brings peace with them...
When they enter the room.
When we are at peace with God,
We are at peace within ourselves...
And that peace can change the atmosphere.

Avoiding things will never bring peace.
Avoiding conflict will never build intimacy.
We will never grow closer to people by avoiding them.
We can't reconcile with others...
If we are afraid to be honest.

We will never grow closer in our marriage...
Or any other relationship by pretending there is no conflict.

Sometimes the best way to engage peace is
To embrace confrontation...
And care enough to help initiate the change needed...
To make peace.
True peace comes through the knowledge...
That God is in control of our circumstances...
And allows only that which is good for us into our life (see
Romans 8:28).

James tells us to consider it joy when a trial comes our way.

It's not that the trial brings joy;
It's what God is doing for us and in us through the trial.
His good work is coming into our lives...
So it can flow out of our lives.

God calls us all to walk in peace...
Thoughtful...humble and mild...
A reflection of His grace...
As an obedient...faithful child.

He wants us to know Him...
And share His forgiveness and His love.
So when we touch another's life...
They'll know it's from above.

May our kindness be a lantern...
Showing others there's no fear.
Let's bring peace and understanding...
To those who need to hear.
Our river of peace..it runs deep...
And will bring healing to their heart.
Peace will ease their heavy burdens...
And still every anxious part.

Peace, so pure and patient...
That flows from the Spirit within...
Shows we love and care...
And leaves the justice up to Him.

God's peace touching earth...
God's love touching man...
Peace flowing like a river...
Is like holding Heaven's hand.

What a comfort, what a mystery...
The peace we'll never understand...
Heaven touching earth...
To bless and still the heart of man.

Power in the Word

Proverbs 13:3, KJV

He that keepeth his mouth keepeth his life: but he that openeth wide his lips shall have destruction.

James 1:26, KJV

If any man among you seem to be religious, and bridleth not his tongue, but deceiveth his own heart, this man's religion is vain.

1 Peter 3:10, NIV

Whoever would love life
and see good days
must keep their tongue from evil
and their lips from deceitful speech.

Proverbs 10:11, KJV

The mouth of a righteous man is a well of life.

God looked down upon the earth.
It was dark...with no form in sight.
He spoke...and started Creation...
With these words, "Let there be light!"

When Abraham went up the mountain to worship...
When the Lord asked him...for Isaac, his son...
He told those travelling with them...
"The lad and I will return when we are done."

God told Moses, "Speak to the Rock"...
And, in anger, he struck it...like he hadn't heard.
God was trying to show him the power
Of the "SPOKEN" Word!

The Shunammite woman who's son died...
Moved in faith and wouldn't tell.
When others questioned what was wrong...
She said, "All is WELL!"

Mary asked "HOW shall this be"...in innocence...
And Zachariah...asked, "HOW"...in doubt.
So the angel shut his mouth...
So nothing negative could come out.

Jesus said to "speak to the mountain"...
And it would be cast into the sea.

Whatever you...believe and say...

That is what...will come to be.

James said our tongue can be a dangerous fire ...

Or can speak blessing instead of strife.

It's up to us the way we speak...

And we bring death or life.

2 Corinthians 4:13, ESV

Since we have the same spirit of faith according to what has been written, "I believed, and so I spoke," we also believe, and so we also speak.

The Power of Choice

Psalm 118:6, ESV

> The LORD is on my side; I will not fear.
> What can man do to me?

Today more than ever...while darkness is covering the earth...
And "gross darkness" the people...
We need to walk in the faith and assurance that God is with us!

This the church's finest hour.
Let's stop whining...and start shining...
For the light of His glory "HAS COME!"

There is fire in the river of God.
It's a river of refreshing and a river of refining!

God is wounding us to heal us.
He's touching us to bring change.
Everything about our lives...
He is going to rearrange.

Until it suits His purpose...
And we are walking in His plan.
This is the only way...
To get to the Promised Land.

We must choose the right way.

At times, my heart is full...
And in happiness I roam...
Not too far this way or that...
But in my "comfort zone."

At times, my heart is heavy...
As doubt steals my faith and sight.
My temper flares...my patience's thin.
And I don't want to do what's right.

At times, my peace is shallow.
I have no energy or will.
I lay around and do "my thing"...
But say...I'm serving Jesus still.

Sometimes I give in way too soon...
And I surrender to my "fate."
I allow my grief to comfort me...
Into a depressed and stagnant state.

At times, my soul and very being...
Walks righteously with God.
He is my Lamp. I follow closely.
With peace my feet are shod.

I long, Lord, to be balanced...
That you would make my footsteps sure...
That my thoughts and notions would align...
To Your eternal spiritual cure.

That double-mindedness would disappear...
And doubt...would leave the scene.
And I would not again be called...
Mr. or Mrs. In-Between.

Quick to Listen

James 1:19-20, NIV

> My dear brothers and sisters, take note of this: Everyone should be quick to listen, slow to speak and slow to become angry, because human anger does not produce the righteousness that God desires.

This applies to all of our relationships...
But, perhaps, it carries the greatest worth...
As we bring this verse to life in our homes.

We all want to leave a strong, vibrant legacy...
To our children and grandchildren.

Do you know that "our words" leave a legacy...
For good or for bad...
Years after we are gone
And for as long as they live in the minds...
Of those we spoke them to and leave behind?

Children will remember, years later,
When we were angry and spoke harshly.
I remember words that were spoken over me still.
They no longer carry power...
Because I have forgiven them...
And replaced them with what God says about me.

Still, we all have a tendency to remember the negative.

It's so wonderful to have our kids and grandkids remember
When we lovingly listened...
And shared in affirming conversation with them.

Every heart is warmed and encouraged...
When we use our words to build and not tear down...
To inspire and not find fault...
To extend grace and not constant criticism.

Listen to understand.
Listen to respond in love.
Let patience and kindness...
Work like a hand and glove.

Be polite and thoughtful...
As you endeavour to walk in their shoes.

When you speak the truth in love...
The devil will always lose.
Words don't go away.
They echo a hurtful sound.
They come from a heart that's unforgiving...
And breeds bitterness all around.

Words are the devil's greatest tool...
That bring damage for years and years.
We must watch the things we say.
They bring pain and future fears.

God is watching over us.
Let His love permeate our life.
And let's quickly forgive each other.
And let go of anger and strife.

May our words have grace.
May our words bring light.
May we always encourage...
And speak what's noble and true and right.

Righteous Judgment

God sees all...and "really knows" all.

Our job is to let God be God and to love and care...

For those that HE has caused...

To be in our lives and part of the family of God.

We are right to warn the Body of believers...

About wrong doctrines and teachings.

However, when we are dealing with a brother and sister...

It is to be in grace and with love...

And ONLY when it involves them actually being "in SIN."

John 7:24, NKJV

> Do not judge according to appearance, but judge with righteous judgment.

Righteous judgment sees SIN for what it is,

And it is not afraid to point it out.

But this judgment will become unrighteous...

When it stems from a "holier than thou" motive...

Or when it seeks to condemn others rather than to restore.

Righteous judgment is "only directed"...

Towards those who are "in SIN."

It is not a license to nit-pick fellow believers...

Acting like we know better about

What they should be doing...

How they should be doing it...

And what we think they could do to improve it.

Galatians 6:1, NIV

> Brothers and sisters, if someone is caught in a sin, you who
> live by the Spirit should restore that person gently. But watch
> yourselves, or you also may be tempted.

"Righteous judgment" is for those...

"Behaving in a carnal manner and in sin."

It is not for those who are living for God...

And doing everything in their power...

To love and serve others.

If we, being someone who is "more spiritual,"

Find a brother or sister in sin...

We are to restore them in a spirit of gentleness.

It should never be in an unrighteous condemning judgment.

A spirit of gentleness...operates by being intentional
About seeking restoration...
And is essential to "righteous judgment."

When we see a fellow Christian "in sin"...
We need to confront the sin...
ONLY IF we have dealt with our own hearts...
Humbly and graciously...
With an understanding...
That we are not above the potential...
To do the very same things.

We are NEVER to judge our brothers and sisters...
"Outside of sin."
We do not judge people.
We judge SIN!

1 John 4:7, NIV

> Dear friends, let us love one another, for love comes from God.
> Everyone who loves has been born of God and knows God.

Many people have struggles.
And some are just too hard to bear.
Imagine living a lonely life...
Having no one who really cares.
We should never judge...

In a hurtful, thoughtless way.
We are called to think about ...
The words we're going to say.

We don't know the things they've suffered...
Or why they wear a mask.
Do we take the time to listen?
Do we take the time to ask?

Correct gently when there's sin...
Not wound with word or stone.
Let's be sure to check our hearts...
That we have no sin of our own.

When I look back on my old life...
There are still tears of great despair.
Thank God for Jesus, my Advocate,
That He is always with me there.

As I cry out, Lord, forgive me...
For the wrong things I still do...
He gently whispers to my heart,
"My child, I died for you."

Righteous Judgment

So, let's not judge another.
Let's celebrate their worth.
We're all God's children...
Through the blessing of rebirth.

Judging creates distance...
Which leads to pain and isolation.
The world cries out for unity...
Not for separation.

Jesus loves us all equally...
And expects us to do the same.
So let's give grace and honour...
In our Saviour's precious name.

Sanctified in Truth

John 17:17, NIV

Sanctify them in the truth; your word is truth.

Psalm 119:160, ESV

The sum of your word is truth,
and every one of your righteous rules endures forever.

Today we have many churches and ministers...
Expounding a false interpretation of the Gospel...
That implies that because God loves us...
It doesn't matter to Him...how we behave.
He has a perfect plan for our perfect and wonderful selves...
And no matter how we might choose to live...
Contrary to HIS TRUTH...He will allow ours...
Because He "made me this way"...
And my behaviour is okay...
And operating out of "my feelings" can't be sinful.
That is a lie. It sounds good...but it's NOT GOD!

Accepting wrong doctrine breeds wrong behaviour.
God is not okay with any kind of sin.
We cannot sanitize or sanctity sin.

Instead of continuing to preach the truth...
And empowering a lifestyle change...by the Spirit...
God has been minimized to a "daddy" who's tolerant...
And accepting of our "sinful personal choices...
And is intent on trying to help us find our "true selves."
God is the same forever. He never changes...
And HE is interested in us being Holy...
And living in HIS TRUTH.

Cultural lies have lulled the church into sanitizing certain sins...
And caused an acceptance to certain violations of God's Word.
We were ALL born into sin...
And, through the born-again process,
We are delivered from it.
THEN we continue to meditate in God's Truth day and night...
That we might not believe "our truth" or the "worlds truth,"
But the ONLY TRUTH, so help me, God!

Today we have used the "love of God" as a way...
To excuse certain sins and actually blame them on God...
Agreeing with the lie that some people were born that way.
Well, we were all "born in sin"...

And chose our rebellious behaviour...
Until we were born again!

God's love is the perfect balance of mercy and justice.
He will not condone and accept any lifestyle choice...
That He calls sin.

It isn't always easy...
To do the thing that's right.
But we must obey the Word of truth...
To be pleasing in God's sight.

Others may be comfortable..
With doing what is wrong.
But we must stay true to our God.
"With Him," we do belong.

His Word must be hidden in our hearts.
We must be filled with Him.
If we'll meditate in His truth...
We will stay away from sin.

When we operate contrarily...
To His Word...we hide.
But we will live in peace and grace..
When "in Him" we abide.

We must always take a stand...
For what is right and true.
The One who matters most...
Lives inside of me and you.

Him alone...we must seek to please.
No one else compares.
For He alone is worthy.
And with us...all things He shares.

No matter what others say and do...
As we stand our ground for Him...
We will always overcome...
And truth will keep us far from sin.

Shine with the Light of the SON

John 8:12, ESV

> Again Jesus spoke to them, saying, "I am the light of the world. Whoever follows me will not walk in darkness, but will have the light of life."

The Lord showed me the sun and the moon...
And said, "The moon has no light of it own.
It reflects the light of the sun.
And when the Earth passes between the sun and the moon,
It grows dark and will eclipse."

He said we are like that moon.
We have no light of our own.
We shine with the light of the "Son."
And when we allow the things of the earth...
To pass between us and His SON...
We cease to shine...
And can have an eclipse of the heart.
A hardening that comes...
That allows our love to wax cold.

Maybe it's our duties...
The things we have to do...every day.
Maybe it's distractions...
Things that we allow to get in the way.
Or divisions with one another...
That strike discord.
Or secret desires and delights...
That...we cannot afford.

We must surrender the man...
Or woman in the mirror every day.
That person is our greatest enemy...
Or our best friend.

Don't let the things of this earth...
Come between your heart and Mine...
So that My love and My light...
Will continue to shine.

If distractions and duties...
Get in the way...
Your heart will eclipse...
And be dark in that day.

If "your delights" take "my place"...
And your affections from Me...
Your vision becomes clouded...
So you cannot see.

The things of the earth...
Will pull us apart.
And you'll have a total...
Eclipse of the heart.

There is NO light...
Outside of Me.
There is no life...
And there never will be.

Shine My light on others.
Share My love and My grace.
Let them "see Me"...
When they look at your face.

Let your eyes have compassion...
When you look at their life...
Remembering the days...
You had heartache and strife...

Understanding and wisdom...
From My heart will flow...
When My mercy and grace...
You continue to show.

But your heart will eclipse...
And darkness will come...
If "things" keep you from shining...
With the "light of the Son."

Speak to Me

What "dwells within" will always produce.

Matthew 12:35, NIV
> A good man brings good things out of the good stored up in him, and an evil man brings evil things out of the evil stored up in him.

When the Word of Christ dwells richly...
Then there will be an outpouring of celebration...
And singing and gratitude from our innermost being...
Unto God.
From the deepest part of our soul...
To the Most High and Almighty One...
Flow rivers of living water.

Our words reveal our heart.
The things we say, and how we say them expose...
And unveil the condition and attitudes of your heart.
Our words set the platform for our actions.

God's sweet presence is more valuable than life.
When we tap into and listen,
We can hear His voice release Heaven's song to our heart.

Lord,
I'm not in a hurry.
I'm waiting. Speak to me.
You hold my every heartbeat...
Now through eternity.

All my times and seasons...
Are measured from Your hand.
Move and change me, Lord...
Like the shifting sand.

You care for me in all the ways...
I desire and need so much.
I feel Your grace and tenderness...
With every word and touch.

One moment with you Lord...
And I'm forever changed.
Basking in Your presence...
I'll never be the same.

There's a special kind of joy...
That only "YOU" can bring.
My heart is full and overflowing.
You are my Everything.

One moment shapes a lifetime...
Making things brand new.
I love being here, Lord...
Caught up in the moment with You.

Suffering

1 Peter 4:12, NIV

> Dear friends, do not be surprised at the fiery ordeal that has come on you to test you, as though something strange were happening to you.

Acts 14:22, NIV

> We must go through many hardships to enter the kingdom of God.

God doesn't deny the suffering in our world.
Instead, He mercifully prepares us for when suffering happens.
He is not just a God who relates to us,
But He is also a God who has taken part in our suffering...
And suffered immensely on our behalf...
Through the cross of Christ.

Suffering reminds us of our humanity...
Of how fragile life can be.

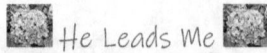

When we go through sickness or loss...
We are reminded that we are not in control of our lives.

If we can see the purpose behind the pain...
We realize that God leverages the suffering in our life...
For greater things.
For greater character...
Greater faith...
Greater dependence upon Him.

Philippians 1:29, NIV

> For it has been granted to "you" on behalf of Christ not only
> to believe in him, but also "to suffer" for him.

Every one of us must deal with the problem of suffering...
Some time in our life.
It's the universal experience of the human race.
We all come into contact with suffering or pain...
Many times during the course of our lives.

Suffering can be very difficult.
It leaves us perplexed and confused...
Often wondering why we have go through this...
Or how God could allow such misery to touch us
Or anyone else.
So many people think God just wants them to be "happy"...

But actually He wants us to be "holy."
We have the joy of the Lord...
That resides on the inside of us...
So that no matter what is happening around us...
We can access the Source of our well-being and strength.

Intimacy with God is often borne in the furnace of affliction.
There's a deeper level of His love that comes...
During times of illness and stress or duress.

My hubby told me that, during the times he suffered...
On his way to healing,
He experienced God in a profound way.
He felt His presence and love in a totally different dimension.

If we choose to rebel against God...
By exercising our will in a contrary way to His...
It can lead to personal suffering.

God is never to blame for the choices we make...
Which lead us to suffering.
Through the gift of our free will...
We get to choose what God says...
Because we love Him and His ways.
Jesus suffered in the garden...
The night before He was to give His life.

He suffered so much, the Bible says,
That He sweat drops of blood.
Yet He submitted to His Father...
And fulfilled God's will for His life...
Becoming the first fruits of many.

The night of the crucifixion...
Peter hit the default button...
And retreated back to the place of his flesh...
Cursing and swearing and denying he even knew Jesus.

1 Peter 4:1, NIV

> Therefore, since Christ suffered in his body, arm yourselves
> also with the same attitude, because whoever suffers in the
> body is done with sin.

Peter didn't want to suffer the persecution...
That would come from admitting...
That he was there...that he knew Jesus.
He didn't want to suffer at the hands of the authorities...
Do he lied...he cussed and he retreated...
To his old way of behaving.

You see, there is a side to suffering we miss...
When we focus only on the pain it causes...
Rather than on God's greater purpose.

Jesus was alone in the garden...
So aware of what He must face.
He was suffering unbearably...
While calling on God's grace.

He cried out to the Father,
"Take this cup from Me.
Not My will but Yours be done.
Father, give Me eyes to see...

That the path that is before Me..
Is Your everlasting plan.
And through the suffering of Your Son...
You will save the souls of man.

God did not promise...
Skies would be ever blue.
He said, "In the midst of the darkness...
I'll be here for you."

God did not promise...
Sun without rain...
Joy without sorrow...
Or peace without pain.

But He has promised us...
Strength from above...
Unfailing compassion...
And undying love.

Thankful for You, Lord

Matthew 13:44, ESV

> The kingdom of heaven is like treasure hidden in a field,
> which a man found and covered up. Then in his joy he goes
> and sells all that he has and buys that field.

Lots of people are completely content...
To have Jesus as Saviour...
Forgiving them of all their sin.
But fewer are ready to have Him as the Lord of their life...
Leading and growing them in godliness.

He is our Saviour...our Lord...and our Treasure.

If we don't love and treasure Jesus...
Then we don't know Him.
Everlasting life in and with Him is simply...
And undeniably worth more than anything else...
We could buy or build or obtain here on earth.

When we fall down...He is there to pick us up.
He's near to the broken and the broken-hearted.

When we feel dry, He pours out His living water...
And the sustenance and strength our soul needs.

At every point that we are weak...
His strength fills us and consumes our weakness...
In order to show the measure of His love and power.

Quietly the shades of evening fall...
Causing shadows across the land.
I hear the sounds of the midnight hour...
And I feel Your loving hand.

The stars shine like diamonds above me.
The heavens are flooded with bright moonlight.
My heart yearns to be with You...
Awake, through the watches of the night.

From my dreams...I will remember...
All the plans You made with me.
And I will awake...and walk them out
Knowing they...will come to be.

Morning...night and noontime...
Warmed by sun...or drenched with rain...
I want You in all seasons...
In the joy and in the pain.

When my soul overflows with passion...
Or I'm downtrodden and depressed...
When I feel alone and heavy laden...
I need the comfort of Your rest.

I need You more that I need anything.
And, as I stand here on life's shore...
I realize that as my life goes on...
I need "You" more and more.

Lord, I want You with me...
Through every changing season.
You're my Song...my Light...my Love...
My Rhyme, and You're my Reason.

I'm so thankful You are with me...
Until the very end...
That You're my Helper and my Comforter...
My Confidante and Friend.

The Kingdom...it belongs to You...
Each and every part.
But You have loved and valued me...
And placed it in my heart.

So my heart...is Your home, Lord.
May it be pleasing in Your sight...
And the place that You find pleasure in...
Morning...noon and night!

The Mirror of His Word

James 1:23-26, NIV

> For if anyone is a hearer of the word and not a doer, he is like a man who looks intently at his natural face in a mirror. For he looks at himself and goes away and at once forgets what he was like. But the one who looks into the perfect law, the law of liberty, and perseveres, being no hearer who forgets but a doer who acts, he will be blessed in his doing. If anyone thinks he is religious and does not bridle his tongue but deceives his heart, this person's religion is worthless.

The beautiful mirror of Gods Word reflects who He is...
And, as we observe and do, we become like Him...
And we reflect His face...
As we dedicate ourselves to a continual coming to the Word...
To inspect and measure ourselves.

As we reflect on the image that we see in God's mirror...
And respond by yielding to the Spirit of grace...
We will see more of Jesus and less of you and me.

As we spend time with Him...we become aware...
That the glory of the Law has faded away...
But the glory of God's grace continues to increase in our lives.

It doesn't matter how hard we try to be obedient.
Obedience will never change human character.

The mirror of God's love and truth is to make us into the image
And likeness of Jesus.
Law may bring us to Jesus...
But only grace can make us like Him.

Every morning we have the glorious chance to begin again.
If we made mistakes yesterday...we can start over...
With a clean slate.

Every new day, hour and breath is filled...
With God's mercy and grace...
Giving us opportunity to bear and display...
More fruit of the Spirit.
Because of His presence within us...
Every day is a new day and another opportunity...
To become more like Him..

We can't gaze into the mirror...
To find out what we lack.

The mirror has no true opinion.
It can't see the way "we act."

It sees only our appearance.
It can know...nothing more.
It sees what's on the outside...
Not what's at our core.

In the flesh...we may look beautiful..,
Polished and upright.
But it's the beauty of the heart...
That is pleasing in God's sight.

The Word of God is "our mirror."
The truth is reflected there...
In the place of love and conviction...
Where He finds our soul laid bare.

Here we find the power...
And the opportunity...
To change the things we need to.
His grace will turn the key.

As I reflect and ask Him questions...
I can feel Him draw me near...
Whispering in words of love...
The things I need to hear.

In this place, my heart is open...
To the things He has to say.
Here I understand...
How to walk fully in His way.

Here, I see within myself...
The truth...I "need" to see.
Here I know my Father...
As He reveals Himself to me.

Here, through revelation,
He gives me eyes to see...
The importance of obedience...
And sweet humility.

Here, I'm mirrored in His presence...
As He fills me to the brim.
Here, in the light of His glory...
I'm made beautiful...like Him!

True Grace

We must love what God loves...and hate what He hates.

He loves a cheerful giver.
He loves justice.
He loves the righteous.
He loves those who obey His commands.
He loves those who pursue godliness.
He loves those who fear Him.

He hates...a proud look.
He hates a lying tongue.
He hates hands that shed innocent blood.
He hates a heart that devises wicked plans.
He hates feet that are swift in running to evil.
He hates a false witness who speaks lies.
He hates the one who sows discord among the brethren.

We live in the days of itching ears...
The feel-good Gospel...

And hyper-grace...
The days where darkness covers the Earth...
And gross darkness the people.

Today, many have made a "graven image" of God...
A God that is acceptable to us...
One we are "willing" to serve...
A "loving" God...who overlooks our sin...
And doesn't require us to repent and confess any longer...
A God who no longer has or exercises "righteous anger"...
A God suitable and satisfactory for us...
One who is admissible...agreeable...and reasonable...
A God who no longer requires us to sacrifice...
Consecrate or set ourselves apart.

We have made for ourselves a God...
Who understands that we are too busy...too tired...
Too overworked...too preoccupied.

The Bible says, "Love the Lord your God
With all your heart and with all your soul
And with all your strength and with all your mind," and...
"Love your neighbour as yourself."
That takes energy and purpose.

But, come on...

I have kids to raise...and a job to do...
A house to look after...and grass to mow too.
I've got laundry to wash...and groceries to buy.
I'll see God on Sunday...or at least I'll "try."
I'm too busy for others...
Not enough hours in the day.
No time for prayer...
But I'm doing okay.
No time for a get-away to the secret place...
But that doesn't matter.
I can just "call on" His "grace."

I don't make enough money...to give to The Lord...
But He understands that I can't afford...
To support what He's doing...His plans and his way.
He understands that I have..."such a small pay."
I have obligations to meet...and a house to pay for.
He knows that I'd give...if I only had more.
My God doesn't require His commands be obeyed.
I mean...I'm in the New. The Old's passed away.
There's freedom to give...what I "feel" to do.
I'm under grace. The Law no longer stands true.
Grace gives me the right to do...what I want to.

My God "is Love." My God is great...always accepting.
My God "doesn't hate." His grace is sufficient...

To "cover my sin." I tell that to my neighbours...
While I sip my tonic and gin.
I can do what I want...what makes me feel good.
It's okay if I don't...though I know that I should.
God will forgive me. I'm just human, you see.
God has no real expectations of me.
He is all loving. He will always forgive.
It's fine with my God...if I live and let live.

My God...is acceptable...tolerant and fair.
He understands...when I'm just not there.
He's reasonable and agreeable...discerning my heart...
Realizing I'm so busy. I just can't take part.
He's admissible and permissive...allowing for my slack...
Always waiting patiently for me to get back on track.
He understands when I'm offended...hurt or mad.
He feels for me when I'm down and sad.
He made me human. He made me this way.
My God loves me...come what may.

My God "tolerates" my bad behaviour.
He doesn't notice when I lie.
He knows I didn't really mean it.
I'm really a good guy.
He overlooks my "opinions"...my emotions and attitude.
He knows my heart. He knows I'm nice...
Though sometimes I'm rude.

My God...is my Comforter. He comes alongside.
He is always wooing me...to come and to abide.
He is always for me...no matter what I do.
It doesn't really matter...what I put others through.
I know...I'm His favourite. I'm His pure and spotless Bride.
It doesn't matter to "my Father"...that I cheated and I lied.

It's true. My God is ever gracious...forbearing...and true.
He always loves His children...no matter what they do.
His grace...it is sufficient...to cover all our mess.
But only when we repent...and are willing to confess.

We must always do our best...to turn from wrong to right.
Always living in His truth...and walking in His light.
My God...He paid the total price...on that dark and dreadful day.
He laid down His life...and took my sin...
To make for me a way...to live my life for Jesus...
And die to that "old man."
He filled me with His Spirit...so He knows I can...
Live a life that's free from sin.
By faith and through His grace...
I'm an overcomer...who reflects my Saviour's face.

But only when I "choose" to...can I walk it out.
Only when I move by faith, not entertaining doubt.
And only when I'm willing...to confess my sin...
Can I be forgiven...turn and come back in.

God's Word hasn't changed...no matter what some may say.
He's the same forever...today and yesterday.

Let's not be deceived...by the doctrines of devils in this hour.
His Word is still the truth, and it carries all of Heaven's power.
Yes, His grace...stands forever.
And His Word is true and right.
Repent...confess...turn once again...
And be "pleasing in His sight."

The Lord says, "I'm looking for the one...
Who gives me her whole life.
I'm looking for a bride...not a common-law wife.
The one who is sold out...and fully fashioned in Me.
I'm looking, Beloved, for intimacy...
Not for someone with so much to do.
I'm looking for love...that is faithful and true...
With all your heart and soul and mind.
Yes, this is the love...this is the kind...
The love that is poured out lavishly...
In the place of intimacy.

I will fully know you...and you will fully know Me.
You will tell me all your secrets...all your troubles and plights...
And, by the power of My Spirit, you will rise up and fight.
And you will be refined in the furnace of My grace.
And others will see Me when they look upon your face.

Your life will tell "My story" and all that I have done...
When you spend some more time basking...
In the glorious Son.

Confession is an admission of weakness...
And, at the same time, a sign of real strength of character.

Matthew 3:8, NLT

Prove by the way you live that you have repented of your
sins and turned to God.

1 John 1:9, NIV

If we confess our sins, he is faithful and just and will forgive
us our sins and purify us from all unrighteousness.

Proverbs 28:13, NIV

Whoever conceals their sins does not prosper,
but the one who confesses and renounces them
finds mercy..

Repentance means I leave the sin...
That I so loved before...
And "show" that I am grieved by it...
By "doing it" NO more.

We Are Our Brother's Keeper

Matthew 25:35-40, NIV

"I was hungry and you gave me something to eat, I was thirsty and you gave me something to drink, I was a stranger and you invited me in, I needed clothes and you clothed me, I was sick and you looked after me, I was in prison and you came to visit me."

Then the righteous will answer him, "Lord, when did we see you hungry and feed you, or thirsty and give you something to drink? When did we see you a stranger and invite you in, or needing clothes and clothe you? When did we see you sick or in prison and go to visit you?"

The King will reply, "Truly I tell you, whatever you did for one of the least of these brothers and sisters of mine, you did for me."

The woman with no coat...
Living on the street...
Has no place to go...
And needs something to eat.

Next time we see her...
Let's not turn away.
WE...can make a difference...
In her life "today."

The little girl in the alley...
Rubbing her eyes...
Is cold and lonely...
So she hides and cries.
Her mommy's addicted.
Her daddy walked away.
WE can make a difference in her life "today."

The troubled teenager...
Thinks no one cares.
At home it's like...
He's not even there.
In a moment of anguish...
He grabs a gun or a knife.
WE could make a difference "today" in his life.

So many struggle...
And fight for their lives.
Alone and lost...
They can barely survive.
The abuse and the pain...

Caused them to stray.
We can make a difference in their life "today."

Out on the streets...
It's freezing cold.
Homelessness affects...
The young and old.
No room...no bed...
No comfort is found.
"Today" we could help turn their lives around.

Isolation and detachment...
Leaves them numb...
Feeling like God...
Is only for "some."
Disheartened and desperate...
They're trying to cope.
Our love in their lives can bring courage and HOPE.

Let's manifest our love...
And DO what we can...
To show the goodness of God...
To our fellowman.
ALL of us...can do our part...
To help a sad and weary heart...
Not just by words...

But by our deeds...
May we bring comfort to those in need.

May we follow Jesus...
In the life we live.
And to those feeling lost...
May we tangibly, generously give..."TODAY."

When we experience cold
And stormy weather conditions...
Imagine how much worse it would be...
For you and me...
If we were on the street!

Let's help "today" by sowing into the lives of those less fortunate.[1]

We Belong

Ephesians 2:19, MSG

You're no longer strangers or outsiders.
You BELONG here.

God wants us all to belong...
To be a part of His family.
When the Body accepts "outsiders" like THEY BELONG...
And makes them feel like THEY BELONG...
It releases grace to them...
And evidences the validity of the Gospel of the love of God.
It gives purpose and meaning and connectivity.

Ephesians 2:19-22, NLT

So now you Gentiles are no longer strangers and foreigners.
You are citizens along with all of God's holy people. You
are members of God's family. Together, we are His
house, built on the foundation of the apostles and
the prophets. And the cornerstone is Christ Jesus

himself. We are carefully joined together in him, becoming a holy temple for the Lord. Through him, you Gentiles [WE] are also being made part of this dwelling where God lives by his Spirit.

We are called to belong,
Not just to believe...
But to "belong to one another"...
And to be those who make others feel like they belong.

When we belong to God...
Brothers and sisters are we...
Working and walking together...
His Body...and Family.

We are one in the Spirit...
Every tribe and tongue and race.
We are called to obey HIS Word...
And live in forgiveness and grace.

When we walk together...
We turn the darkness to light.
When we care for one another...
We are pleasing in God's sight.
Our spiritual Family is Heaven-sent...
Chosen by our Father above...
Every member called as one..
And bonded by His love.

We learn to stand with one another...
Not point fingers and place blame...
Always willing to believe and pray...
In Jesus' precious name.

We learn to walk in mercy and goodness...
With wisdom and understanding...
With patience and kindness...
Never pushy and demanding.

We may be rejected...
By those who do not care.
When we feel cast down...
Our family's always there.

And we learn to love in spite of...
And not because of anything...
One in heart and spirit...
With our Lord and King.

Your Word Gives Me Wings

Hebrews 4:12, NIV

For the word of God is alive and active. Sharper than any
double-edged sword, it penetrates even to dividing soul
and spirit, joints and marrow; it judges the thoughts and
attitudes of the heart.

When we go to God's Word...we go to discover Him.
He is the prize. He is the goal.
In discovering more of who He is...
We discover more of who we are.

To fill God's prescription for abundant life...divine health...
And overcoming power we must diligently attend...
To His Word.
We must give HIS Word (Jesus) the first place of authority...
In our life and spend time with Him every day...
Remembering that the more we know the Word...
The more we know the Person of Jesus.

The forces of life and power that come out of our heart ...
Will be in direct proportion to the amount of HIS Word...
That actively lives in us.

We can't overdose on God's life medicine.
In fact...the more Word we take...the stronger we become.
We have nothing to lose but sickness and disease...
Poverty. loss and pain.
And we have so much to gain.

Today, let's begin taking God's medicine daily...
A liberal dose of His Word...
And putting it to work in our lives.
It's our personal prescription for life and health...
And a recipe for life and life abundant.

His Word...is "our wings."

You broke my chains of sin and shame...
And covered me with grace.
You refine my life with holy fire...
Till I reflect Your face.

You touch me and You change me.
You constantly renew...
Until I am transformed...
And I look just like You.

You draw me into the secret place...
And, by Your Spirit, You impart...
Your life and personality...
So I will have Your heart.

You constantly remind me...
By the conviction of Your Spirit...
That I need to "walk out" Your Word...
And not just simply "hear it."

Your Word gives me wings.
Your Word changes things.
What great peace it brings!
Your Word gives me wings.

It teaches me about your grace.
It turns me from all sin.
It sets me free to soar on high.
And empowers me to win.

It Instructs me that repentance...
Is the way to constant change...
As You perfect in me Your character...
You take out...and rearrange...

Everything that does not please You.
Till I have peace in place of strife...
The Carpenter's job is not complete.
Until I am living out "Your life."

I must die to my own way...
And be lost to my own plan.
Then I will walk in the fear of God...
And not the fear of man.

Keeping my heart soft before you...
Repentant...in all my ways...
Staying free from unforgiveness...
All my earthly days.

Your Word gives me wings.
Your Word changes things.
What great peace it brings!
Your Word gives me wings.

Your Word...it will change me.
It's a mirror to my soul.
Making me into the Bride of Christ...
Is Your Word's...highest goal.

I will be pleasing and lovely...
As I'm washed with the water of grace.
And my life will be a testimony...
As my life reflects Heaven's face.

YOUR WORD GIVES ME WINGS

You're More than Enough

Psalm 139:14, NIV

> I praise you because I am fearfully and wonderfully made;
>> your works are wonderful,
>> I know that full well.

You're more than enough.
You are one of a kind.
You're unique and classic...
With a quick and sharp mind.

Your smile's contagious.
Your personality's bright.
You're kind and compassionate.
You shine with His light.

But at times you feel down...
Believing you're not enough...
Thinking you can't overcome...
When circumstances seem rough.

When you get to that place...
Just remember what's true:
No one else has the call...
To do what God's called you to do.
You're perfect to Him.
You are His light in the dark.
You're full,of life...and alert.
You won't miss the mark.

You are more than enough.
Yes, you're one of a kind.
You're a beautiful treasure...
A rare and valuable find.

You are more than enough.
You're chosen and called.
With your life and success...
God's committed...enthralled.

He wants us to be tender...
Even when love seems so tough.
But in every situation...
He says that we're enough.

Author Contact Page

You may contact the author in the following ways:

By Email
mave @ eagleworldwide.com

By Phone:
+1 850 748 0895

By Mail:
PO Box 39
Copetown ON L0R1J0
Canada

On Facebook:

facebook.com / eagleworldwide

facebook.com / russ_and_mave_moyer

By visiting his website:
www.EagleWorldwide.com

EAGLE WORLDWIDE RETREAT & REVIVAL CENTRE

SUMMER CAMP TENT REVIVAL

July through August
8 Powerful Weeks of Revival
Every Night @ 7:00 pm

Specialty Schools
School of the Prophets
School of Freedom and Healing
School of the Supernatural

Location: 976 Hwy 52 Copetown ON L0R 1J0
Call for more details 905 308 9991
www.EagleWorldwide.com

WINTER CAMP REVIVAL GLORY

February/March
10 Powerful Days of Revival Glory
Every Night @ 7:00 pm

Specialty Schools
School of the Prophets

The Dwelling Place
7895 Pensacola Blvd Pensacola FL 32534
Call for more details 850 473 8255
www.TheDwellingPlaceChurch.org

EAGLE WORLDWIDE NETWORK

CREDENTIALING & SPIRITUALLY COVERING

Ministers
Marketplace Ministers
Traveling & Itinerant Ministers
Missionaries
Churches
Church Networks
Home Churches
Outreach Ministries
And more...

GOVERNING OFFICIAL
PASTOR MAVE MOYER

NETWORK COORDINATOR
PASTOR JOANNA ADAMS

CREDENTIALS AVAILABLE

Certified Practical Minister
Licensed Minister
Ordained Minister

OFFICE@EAGLEWORLDWIDE.COM

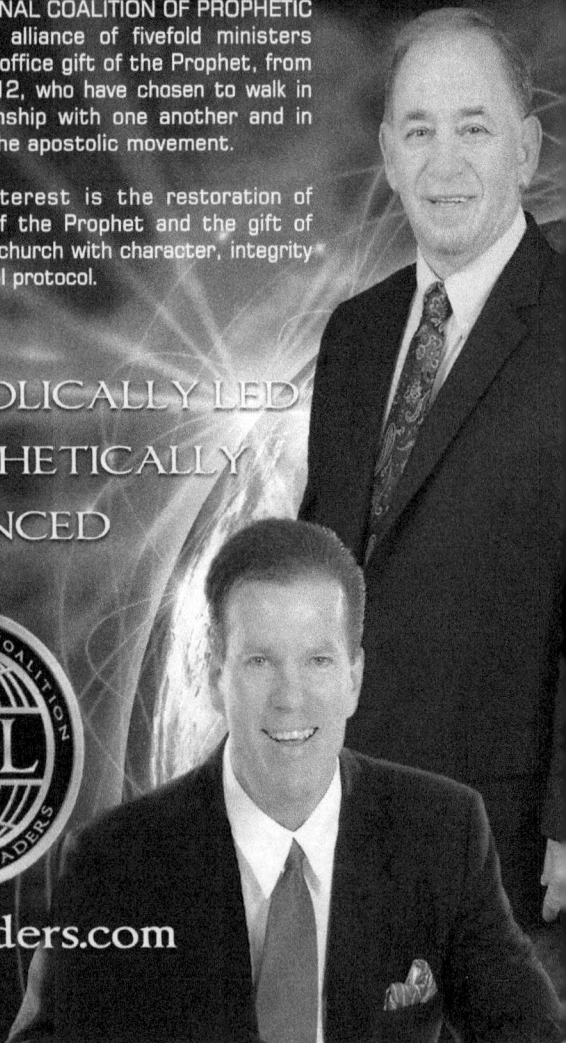

EAGLE WORLDWIDE
The COMMUNITY ENRICHMENT
KING'S
WAY
Our dedicated team of volunteers work together to provide...
Hot Meals
Clothing
Toiletries & Basic Household Items
We also provide quality programming designed to
EMPOWER & EQUIP
individuals to have a better quality of life and make a
POSITIVE IMPACT in their community.
The King's Way
649 King Street East
Hamilton . ON . L8N 1E5
Centre 905 296 9473
ALifeAtATime.com
TRANSFORMING OUR COMMUNITY
A LIFE AT A TIME!

www.ingramcontent.com/pod-product-compliance
Lightning Source LLC
LaVergne TN
LVHW051225080426
835513LV00016B/1425